Instructor's M

MW01520539

Cooking Essentials for The New Professional Chef™

The Food and Beverage Institute

MARY DEIRDRE DONOVAN

Editor

VAN NOSTRAND REINHOLD

I(T)P® A Division of International Thomson Publishing Inc.

New York • Albany • Bonn • Boston • Detroit • London • Madrid • Melbourne
Mexico City • Paris • San Francisco • Singapore • Tokyo • Toronto

Copyright © 1997 by The Culinary Institute of America

Published by Van Nostrand Reinhold

I(T)P® A division of International Thomson Publishing Inc.
The ITP logo is a registered trademark under license

Printed in the United States of America

For more information, contact:

Van Nostrand Reinhold
115 Fifth Avenue
New York, NY 10003

Chapman & Hall GmbH
Pappelallee 3
69469 Weinheim
Germany

Chapman & Hall
2–6 Boundary Row
London
SE1 8HN
United Kingdom

International Thomson Publishing Asia
221 Henderson Road #05-10
Henderson Building
Singapore 0315

Thomas Nelson Australia
102 Dodds Street
South Melbourne, 3205
Victoria, Australia

International Thomson Publishing Japan
Hirakawacho Kyowa Building, 3F
2-2-1 Hirakawacho
Chiyoda-ku, 102 Tokyo
Japan

Nelson Canada
1120 Birchmount Road
Scarborough, Ontario
Canada M1K 5G4

International Thomson Editores
Seneca 53
Col. Polanco
11560 Mexico D.F. Mexico

All rights reserved. No part of this work covered by the copyright hereon may be reproduced or used in any form or by any means—graphic, electronic, or mechanical, including photo-copying, recording, taping, or information storage and retrieval systems—without the written permission of the publisher.

1 2 3 4 5 6 7 8 9 10 PAT 01 00 99 98 97 96

ISBN 0-442-02464-9

http://www.vnr.com

product discounts   free email newsletters
software demos   online resources

email: info@vnr.com

A service of I(T)P®

Introduction

This instructor's manual has been prepared so that you can use it to suit a wide variety of curriculums and teaching styles. As you look through its pages, you will notice the following elements:

1. CHAPTER OBJECTIVES

These are the same objectives stated in the text itself. We have also included page references to help you locate the exact section of the text that covers the topic.

2. CHAPTER OUTLINES

We have compiled the contents of each chapter into major headings and subheadings, to act as a guide when preparing your classroom lectures. Use your own curriculum and class times to determine how much material you need for each day's lecture. For some of the larger chapters, the outlines have been broken down into specific topics.

Whenever appropriate, short numbered or bulleted lists have been incorporated into the outline to act as a quick, on-the-spot reference to basic information from the book.

3. DISCUSSION TOPICS AND ASSIGNMENTS

There are a number of ways to help students delve deeper into any given topic. The activities in the book are a good place to look. In this guide we have included a number of related topics for use to generate in-class discussions, brainstorming sessions, and out-of-class written assignments.

While there are no definitive answers provided, we have suggested some basic elements that you can use to either jump start discussions or gauge how well your students are assimilating the material.

4. KEY TERMS WITH DEFINITIONS

You can use this to test mastery of the language used in the professional kitchen during in-class question and answer sessions, or incorporate these terms into pop quizzes or a section in larger tests that you may administer to your class.

5. ANSWERS TO SELF-STUDY QUESTIONS

Each chapter in the book includes a number of self-study questions that can be used either to review material or to test mastery. If you assign these questions as homework or include them on tests, you can look here for some elements that you might like to see in the response that your students return to you.

Throughout the guide, we have provided resources you might use in your teaching. We have included organizations, books, magazines (in some cases cited the specific feature or column), and videos that can offer more information or a fresh perspective on a given topic.

In the back of the manual, we have incorporated some overhead "masters" that can be duplicated.

We invite your comments and suggestions about additional materials you would find useful. Please direct your comments to the Editors.

Introduction to the Profession

Objectives

- Discuss some of the key historical events and figures that shaped the modern foodservice industry (pages 2–3)
- Trace the history and evolution of restaurants (pages 3–5)
- Explain the influence of society and its structure, science and technology, and nutrition on the development of the food service industry (pages 6–8)
- Identify some of the first American chefs who began to define our national cuisine (page 5)
- Understand how science and technology have affected the modern foodservice industry (page 6)
- Identify some of the most significant currents and trends in today's foodservice industry (page 6)

Lecture Outline

INTRODUCTION TO THE PROFESSION
A HISTORICAL PERSPECTIVE
   Royalty and the Rise of the Middle Class
RESTAURANT HISTORY
THE EVOLUTION OF RESTAURANT CUISINES
   Grande Cuisine
   Classic Cuisine
   Nouvelle Cuisine
   American Cuisine
   Into the Future
Sidebar *Major Historical Figures*
TODAY'S CURRENTS AND TRENDS
   Science and Technology
      Hybridization
      Animal husbandry

   Nutrition
   Family Structure Changes
   Media and the Information Superhighway
SUMMARY

Discussion Topics

TOPIC: Contemporary chef profiles as trendsetters and role models:
- Alice Waters
- Madeline Kammen
- Mark Miller
- Freddy Giradet
- Susan Spicer
- Charlie Trotter
- Rick Bayless

- Susan Feniger
- Mary Sue Milliken
- Claude Troisgros
- Larry Forgione
- Jasper White
- Dean Fearing
- Marcel Desaulnier
- Jeremiah Tower
- André Soltner

Ways to Approach Topic

Solicit examples from students (could be homework assignment or "top of the head"). Give brief background lecture or hand out material to students.

Resource: Video

Great Chefs VideoTape Series. *Culinary Institute of America,* 1995, 1996.

Resource: Magazines

Food Arts, including, "Front Burner," "Say Cheese," and "Silver Spoon Award," monthly features
Art Culinaire
Chef, including "Chef Spotlight" and "Chefs on the Move" monthly features
Food and Wine, including "Experts," monthly feature

TOPIC: Historical and current food trends
- *Grande cuisine*
- *Nouvelle cuisine*
- American cuisine
- Fusion
- Pacific rim
- Mediterranean

TOPIC: Impact of science, technology and agriculture
- Aquaculture
- Irradiation
- Biological engineering/genetic altering
- Biotechnology

- Hydroponics
- Boutique farmers
- Organic farming
- Animal husbandry

Additional material for this chapter may be found in the back of this manual. See "Code of Ethics for Professional Culinariens," "Take Time for Success," and "Feedback."

Assignments

1 The kitchen is very busy. It is Saturday night and the dining room is crowded with customers. Customers are waiting a long time for their food. When an unhappy guest gets up to complain, he looks in the kitchen and sees that everyone is running around and that no one seems to know who is doing what. Offer possible reasons for the situation as well as ways to resolve the problem.

  Situation, e.g.:

- Not enough *mise en place* prepared
- Not enough staff
- Staff not properly trained
- Bad organization
- Too many reservations seated at same time

  Solutions:

- Chef should delegate some responsibilities to sous chef
- Organize in the morning:
    Take inventory
    Review other Saturday nights to determine needs
    Make mise en place prep list
- Provide training for front-of-house and back-of-house

2 Sometimes, in discussions, it helps to look at something from the opposite point of view. For example, consider how you could fail. As the chef of a family restaurant, what kind of items could you put on your menu that would undoubtedly fail. Why?

Examples:

- Game items
- Offal
- Foie gras
- Caviar

Why:

- Expense
- Not familiar
- Not popular with children
- Staff not skilled enough to prepare them
- See also pages 5–7.

3 Brainstorming: We are all occasionally customers in restaurants. What experiences have you had that have given you a very negative or a very positive impression? What are your personal restaurant pet peeves? What have you learned from these experiences that you can apply to your own development as a professional?

Answer Key to Self-Study Questions

1 By bringing together from different cultures:
- Ingredients
- Cooking tools
- Techniques
- Social customs associated with eating

2 The evolution of Western cuisine since the 1800s has loosely included the following chronology:
  (1) Eighteenth-century *grande cuisine,* contributions from Carême and Brillat-Savarin
  (2) Nineteenth-century classic cuisine, with the most significant contributions from Escoffier
  (3) Early-to mid-twentieth-century *nouvelle cuisine,* with major contributions from Fernand Point, Paul Bocuse, Alain Chapel, Françoise Bise, and the Troisgros brothers
  (4) Late twentieth-century contemporary "American" cuisine with major contributions from, among others, Larry Forgione, Jeremiah Tower, Alice Waters, and Dean Fearing

3 Parisian tavern owner who, in the late 1760s, served a dish called a *restorante* (restorative), which evolved into the term "restaurant" that we use today.

4 Brillat-Savarin—politician, gourmet and author of *Le Physiologie de Gout (The Physiology of Taste).*
  la Varenne—author of the first cookbook of the French nobility, *Le Vrai Cuisinier François,* 1651.
  Escoffier—author of *Le Guide Culinaire,* devised the present day brigade system and widely regarded as the grandfather of modern Western cuisine.

5 Greater demand for:
- Carry-out cuisine
- Early-bird specials
- Faster service
- Light and vegetarian menu selections at fine restaurants
- Delicious and nutritious value meals
- More variety for families that eat out a lot
- Expanded selection of kids' menu offerings

6 She brought:
- A more refined style of eating
- Sophisticated table manners
- Indigenous Italian food products, including spinach

7 Farming:
- Aquaculture
- Animal husbandry
- Chemical fertilizers
- Hybridization
- Seed banks

Technologies:
- Stoves
- Microwaves
- Computerized kitchen equipment
- Additives/preservatives
- Pasteurization
- Freeze-drying
- Vacuum packing
- Irradiation

Keywords

à la carte (Fr.): A menu in which the patron makes individual selections from various menu categories.

American cuisine: A cooking style featuring the foods, dishes, and cooking styles indigenous to various parts of the United States.

Animal husbandry: The practice of breeding and raising a variety of farm animals so as to maximize production of meat, dairy, and eggs.

Brigade system: The kitchen organization system instituted by Auguste Escoffier. Each position has a station and well-defined responsibilities.

Carte (Fr.): The general term for menu or listing.

Cuisine bourgeoisie (Fr.): The cooking style of the middle class.

Freeze-drying: A food preservation method.

Grande cuisine (Fr.): A cooking style established by Antonin Carême, detailed in *La Cuisine Classique.*

Haute cuisine (Fr.): "High cuisine." The cooking style of the upper class.

Hybridization: Breeding technique in which plant strains are developed in such a way that specific traits are minimized or maximized.

Irradiation: Food preservation technique in which foods are made shelf-stable by exposure to low doses of radiation.

Nouvelle cuisine (Fr.): "New cooking." A culinary movement emphasizing freshness and lightness of ingredients, classical preparations, and innovative combinations and presentation.

Pasteurization: A process in which milk products are heated to kill microorganisms that could contaminate the milk.

Restaurant: A business in which foods are prepared and served to a paying customer.

Table d'hôte (Fr.): A fixed-price menu with a single price for an entire meal based on entrée selection.

Vacuum packing: A system of packing foods in a closed environment, with as much air as possible removed.

CHAPTER 1

The Professional Chef

Objectives

- Define the important personal attributes of a professional chef (pages 17–18)
- Explain the importance of a good basic education as well as continuing education to the professional chef (pages 14–15)
- Name the positions in a classic brigade system for the kitchen and dining room (pages 18–20)
- Name several possible career options in the foodservice industry (pages 21–22)
- Explain how to network and why networking is important for a strong career in the foodservice industry (page 31)
- Define the chef's role as an executive, administrator, and manager (pages 22–30)
- Explain the significance of marketing to a restaurant's success (pages 32–34)

Lecture Outline

BECOMING A CRAFTSMAN
  Getting an Education
  Continuing Education
    Nutrition
    Food Safety Issues
    Organic Foods
    Environmental Concerns
    Vegetarianism
A CHEF'S PROFESSIONAL AND PERSONAL
ATTRIBUTES
  A Commitment to Service
  A Sense of Responsibility
  Judgment
  Looking the Part

CAREER PATHS FOR PROFESSIONALS IN
FOODSERVICE
  Kitchen Brigade System
  Sidebar The Dining Room Brigade System
  Types of Restaurants and Other Foodservice
  Establishments
  Alternative Careers In Foodservice
THE CHEF AS EXECUTIVE, ADMINISTRATOR, AND
MANAGER
  Becoming a Good Executive
  Becoming a Good Administrator
  Becoming a Good Manager
    Managing Physical Assets
  Sidebar Managing Time
    Controlling Food Cost

Discussion Topics

TOPIC: Avenues for interacting with the community
- Environmental concerns
  Impact on the environment of purchasing and use of food, paper goods, and equipment
  Recycling
  Farmer's markets or cooperatives (consult local agencies, newspapers, or community groups)
  Organic farming

Resource: Organization

Chef's Collaborative 2000
Oldways Preservation and Exchange Trust
45 Milk Street
Boston, MA 02109
(617) 695-9102

- Providing food, service, and education to the local community

Resource: American Service Organizations

Food Chain: The network of prepared and perishable food-rescue programs
970 Jefferson Street, NW
Atlanta GA 30318
(800) 845-3008

Chefs in America Foundation
3407 Toledo Street
Coral Gables, FL 33134
(305) 448-9279

Share Our Strength
1511 K Street, NW
Suite 94
Washington, DC 20005
(202) 393-2925

TOPIC: Mentoring/Volunteering/Fundraising: This could be a brainstorming project. Break the class into smaller groups or do as single group. List as many ways a chef can reach out to help others as possible.

TOPIC: Networking and Promotion
- Professional organizations, see page 786
- Internet
- Continuing education demos, as student or instructor
- Conferences/festivals
- Benefits/volunteer/fundraise/mentor (benefits the chef, as well)
- Competitions/food shows (local, regional, national, international)
- Media: journalism, tv, radio (e.g. TVFN, local access, etc.)

Resource: Magazines

Food Arts, including "Events Calendar" and "Say Cheese," monthly features
Chef, "Calendar," monthly feature
Saveur, "Agenda," monthly feature

TOPIC: Resume Writing

Resource: Books

Dynamic Cover Letters. Randall Hanson and Katharine Hanson. Ten Speed Press. Berkeley, CA, 1990.

Resume Pro: The Professional Guide. Yana Parker, Ten Speed Press. Berkeley, CA, 1993.

Top Secret: Resume and Cover Letters. Steven Provenzano. Dearborn Financial Publishing, Inc., Chicago, 1995.

TOPIC: Interviewing Techniques

Resource: Books

Interviewing: Effective Techniques To Help You Answer Tough Questions and Make a Great Impression. Arlene S. Hirsch. John Wiley & Sons, Inc., New York, 1994.

Your First Interview: Everything You Need To Know To "Ace" The Interview Process and Get Your First Job. Ronald W. Fry. Career Press. Hawthorne, NJ, 1991.

TOPIC: Communications
• Methods of communication spoken and written
  Nonverbal
  Active listening

Resource: Video

Improving Communication Skills. *Educational Institute of the American Hotel and Motel Association,* 1991, (800) 752-4567.

TOPIC: Total Quality Management (TQM)

Resource: Books

The Five Pillars of TQM. Bill Creech. Truman Tally Books/Dutton. New York, 1994.

Taking the Mystery Out of TQM. Peter Capezio and Debra Morehouse. Career Press. Hawthorne, NJ, 1993.

TOPIC: Personnel Issues
• EEO
• Sexual Harassment

Resource: Video

Myth vs. Fact: How to Recognize and Confront Subtle Sexual Harrasment. *BNA Communications (Bureau of National Affairs, Inc.),* 1994, (301) 948-0540.

• Employee benefits/know your rights as employee and employer

Resource: Books

Wages and Benefits for Salaried Employees and Executives in Foodservice. National Restaurant Association. NRA in Association with Laventhol & Horwath. Washington, DC, 1988.

Managing for Productivity in the Hospitality Industry. Robert Christie Mill. Van Nostrand Reinhold. New York, 1989.

• Managing diversity
  family status, age, race, religion, sexual orientation
  encouraging personal growth and development

Resource: Book

Voices of Diversity: Real People Talk About Problems and Solutions in a Workplace Where Not Everyone is Alike. Renee Blank and Sandra Slip. American Management Association (AMACOM). New York, 1994.

TOPIC: Noncooking skills of the chef:
• Supervising

Resource: Books

Supervision in the Hospitality Industry. Mary Porter and Karen Eich Drummond. FMP, John Wiley & Sons, Inc., New York, 1992.

What Every Supervisor Should Know. Lester Bittel and John Newstrom. Macmillan/McGraw-Hill. New York, 1990.

- Communicating (in house and with outside)
- Teaching/training/educating/being educated
- Computer knowledge, on-line and recipe/costing/inventory programs, nutritional analysis, networking, information gathering, payroll, mailing lists, reservation systems

Resource: Magazine

Food Arts, "Tech Talk," bimonthly feature

Resource: Video

Recipe Costing: The Bottom Line. *Culinary Institute of America,* 1996.

Resource: Book

Controlling and Analyzing Costs in Food Service Operations/3e. J. Keiser and F. J. DeMicco. Macmillan, New York, 1993.

TOPIC: Teambuilding: Managing front and back of house
- Role-playing
- Cross training: make the chef be manager or waiter one day, have the waiters work behind the line

TOPIC: Alternative careers in food

Resource: Book

Careers for Gourmets & Others Who Relish Food. Mary Donovan. VGM Career Horizons. Chicago, 1993.

Resource: Video

Culinary Careers: People, Professionalism, Service. *The American Culinary Federation, 1988.*

Resource: Organization

International Association of Culinary Professionals
304 West Liberty
Suite 201
Louisville, KY 40202
(502) 581-9786
Additional material for this chapter may be found in the back of this manual. See "Cooking Guidelines" and "Weights and Measures"

Resource: Magazine

Food Arts, "Tech Talk," bimonthly feature

Assignments

1 "Yes, buying organic vegetables is good for P.R., but there's a much bigger issue we're trying to deal with." (Daniel Leader, Bread Alone.) What is the "bigger issue" to which Daniel Leader is referring?
- Environment
- Health
- See also pages 16–17.

2 When purchasing food and nonfood stock, you must weigh the cost of environmentally safe products with the benefits of using them. How can you pass the costs on to your customers in a way that will satisfy everyone?
- Promote the use of those products that are safe for the environment—good public relations
- Try to reduce costs in other areas so that prices do not increase
- See also pages 16–17.

3 Several customers complained when they received their takeout coffee in styrofoam cups. When the owner began using paper cups, the customers complained about the price increase. What should the owner do?
- See Question 2 above. Owner should promote environment-friendly items and practices, perhaps offer discount to customers who bring in their own coffee cups.
- See also pages 16–17.

4 Some of the chefs in the area want to establish a local food bank for the homeless. Discuss some of the problems in organizing such an operation. Discuss the benefits.

Problems:

- Public perception of homeless—difficult to change
- Alleviating concern over liability (good samaritan law)
- Cost (many corporations are getting involved and donating money for food rescue)
- Equipment
- Organizing labor (usually volunteer)

Benefits:

- No waste
- Public relations: good for business: celebrities and restaurants are hosting events to raise money for such operations
- Personal benefits: helps others, feels good, perhaps cuts down on theft, and panhandling, and you can direct persons in need where to go for foods

5 Brainstorming: Discuss several issues with the following scenerio:
Two couples are leaving a restaurant where they have had dinner. They are discussing their evening. The women felt uncomfortable in the dining room, but they cannot explain exactly why. Both couples wonder why they felt they were eating so quickly. One of the men says that the music was too loud and a little too modern for his taste. None of them wanted to linger after dinner for coffee.

- Music was too loud and perhaps inappropriate
- Service was too fast
- May be a problem only from the customers' point of view. They may have chosen the wrong restaurant; this is a popular restaurant but suited for a "younger" customer
- See also pages 32, 34.

6 What is total utilization? Give some examples of how it works in a kitchen.

e.g. Chicken purchased whole used for:
- Bones in the stock
- Juices in the sauce
- Dark meat in the soup
- Breast as the entrée
- Unsold cooked breast added to soup

Lobster purchased whole used for:

- Meat, 50%—salad, Newburg
- Carcass, 50%—make broth or bisque
  Although the following will not yield profits, they are preferable to garbage:
- Leftovers to food bank
- Compost to farmers
- See also pages 23–29, 33.

7 Divide class into groups. Give each group 15 minutes to name as many food careers as they can that do not involve cooking in a kitchen. Discuss the variety of responses.
- See also pages 21–22.

Answer Key to Self-Study Questions

1 • Make a commitment to providing the best possible service to guests
- Cultivate responsible behavior and healthy self-esteem within oneself
- Take pride in all the work done as a professional chef

2 • Attend an accredited school
- Receive on-the-job training with experienced chefs
- Work as an apprentice in an apprenticeship program or a self-directed course of study

3 • Sauté station—sautéed items and sauces
- Fish station—fish items (maybe butchering and sauces)
- Roast station—roast and sauces
- Grill station—grilled food
- Fry station—fried food
- Vegetable station (and soup station)—hot appetizers (may be soups, vegetables, starches, and pasta)
- Roundsman—swing cook
- Commis—assistant, trains on any station

4   • Track inventory
    • Submit purchase orders to purveyors
    • Nutritional analysis
    • Recipe costing
    • Recipe scaling (for greater or fewer numbers of servings)
    • Recipe conversion (from metric to U.S.)
    • Create menus
    • Track salaries
    • Reservations
    • Assist in maintaining accurate business records
    • Information gathering and networking

5   • Organic agriculture
    • Solid waste disposal
    • Composting
    • Recycling
    • Food handling
    • Foodborne illnesses

6   "Organic"—living, natural matter is used to enrich the soil, control pests, and enhance yields, rather than using chemical fertilizers, pesticides, and steroids.

    Importance to chef:
    • Future integrity of food products is at stake if we do not support the proper care of food-producing soils over the long-term
    • Public is increasingly seeking out and supporting organic food products on menus
    • Cost for most organic items is still higher, which affects the chefs' food cost calculations and purchasing decisions

7   Physical assets—the items that you must purchase or pay for to run a profitable restaurant:
    • Food and beverage
    • Utilities
    • Waste removal
    • Taxes
    • Insurance
    • Rent
    • Mortgage or lease payments
    • Tables and chairs
    • Linens
    • China
    • Flatware
    • Glassware
    • Computers
    • Cash registers
    • Pots and pans
    • Other kitchen equipment
    • Cleaning supplies and/or service.

8   (a) The amount of stock (inventory) you should have consistently available to cover operating needs between deliveries.
    (b) Having too much stock ties up valuable space, while not having enough stock can make it impossible to produce a given menu item.

9   "As purchased/AP" is the cost of food when it is received.
    "Edible Portion/EP" is the cost of food once it is properly processed, prior to cooking.
    Divide EP by AP to determine how much the food you serve your guests actually costs. This information can be used to establish menu pricing standards and food cost controls to ensure that a profit is made.

10 (1) Develop a list of needs
    (2) Develop quality and purchasing specification
    (3) Select purveyors
    (4) Organize a delivery schedule
    (5) Develop a parstock
    (6) Take purchase inventory
    (7) Forecast contingency needs
    (8) Take market quotes
    (9) Maintain a purchase log

11 (1) Factor method: cost of food sold should equal a specified percentage of the sales in dollars.
    (2) Prime cost: raw food, labor, and operating costs are each assigned a percentage of total dollar expenditures, which are then used to calculate a menu price.
    (3) Actual cost: actual cost of raw ingredients, plus actual payroll and additional labor costs, plus all the fixed and variable expenses associated with operating a restaurant, plus an allowance figure for profit, totaled together will give you the menu price.

12
- Customer base
- Menu design
- Restaurant design and ambiance
- Style of service provided

13 Proper training for service staff at all levels.

Keywords

Actual cost: A determination of an item's cost that must include cost of raw materials, labor, overhead, and any other operating expense related to that item's procurement and eventual sale.

As purchased/AP: The weight of an item before trimming or other preparation (as opposed to edible portion weight or EP).

Code of conduct: A standard (which may be expressed or simply understood) governing actions deemed suitable to those within a group, organization, or profession.

Brigade system: The kitchen organization system instituted by Auguste Escoffier. Each position has a station and well-defined responsibilities.

Cost of errors: A calculation of the total expenses involved in improperly serving or preparing an item intended for sale to the customer.

Edible portion/EP: The weight of an item after trimming and preparation (as opposed to the as purchased weight or AP).

Factor method: A system used to determine the menu price of various items.

Food cost: Cost of all food purchased to prepare items for sale in a restaurant.

Marketing: The process by which potential customers are made aware of the services, goods, or potential value of something in order to encourage them to buy or invest.

Menu development: Planning and writing a menu to meet general standards and requirements of an individual operation.

Menu price: Selling price determined by calculating various costs associated with producing an item.

Organic foods: Foods raised without chemical fertilizers, herbicides, pesticides, artificial growth hormones, or antibiotics. Standards vary.

Pantry: The area of the kitchen responsible for breakfast, sandwich, and salad preparation.

Prep cook: Usually the first job a novice or new-hire holds in a kitchen; typically responsible for preparing vegetables, tending stocks, and other advance preparation tasks.

Prime cost: Menu pricing method in which percentages are assigned to cover raw food, direct labor, and operating costs involved in food preparation and service.

Professional network: A personal or public group of individuals who share a common profession; used to gather information, job search, placement, etc.

Purchasing: The act of buying raw goods necessary to perform work or provide a service.

Quality service: Providing service that meets standards of quality based on the restaurant and menu type as well as the particular establishment's standards and needs.

Sous chef (Fr.): Under-chef. The chef who is second in command in a kitchen; usually responsible for scheduling, filling in for the chef, and assisting the chefs de partie as necessary.

Standard portion (or serving) sizes: Serving sizes based on calorie and nutrient requirements.

Standardized recipes: Recipes written according to standards determined by an operation to assure consistent cooking, garnish, and service procedures.

Toque blanche (Fr.): "White hat." A chef's hat.

C H A P T E R   2

Food and Kitchen Safety

Objectives

- List the three ways in which foods can become contaminated and name some of the strategies for avoiding contamination in the kitchen (pages 41–43)
- Name different types of foodborne illnesses, their sources, and symptoms (pages 40–41)
- Explain what is meant by potentially hazardous foods (page 43)
- Define danger zone and name several critical temperatures in safe food-handling practices (page 44)
- Understand the connection between personal hygiene and the prevention of foodborne illness (pages 50–52)
- Learn to apply the correct procedures for cooling and reheating foods (pages 45–49)
- Explain HACCP (pages 48–50)
- Name several key points for keeping the kitchen safe and sanitary (pages 52–56)

Lecture Outline

SAFE FOODS
   A Safe Food Supply
TYPES OF FOODBORNE DISEASES
   1. Food Intoxication
   2. Food Infection
   Staphylococcus
   Salmonellosis
   Trichinosis
   Botulism
   Toxic Poisioning
REDUCING THE RISK OF FOODBORNE ILLNESS
   Chemical Contamination in the Kitchen
   Physical Contamination in the Kitchen
   Biological Contamination

Potentially Hazardous Foods
The Three Requirements of Pathogens
   Protein
   Water
   Moderate pH
THE DANGER ZONE
   Temperature
   Time
   1. Lag Phase
   2. Accelerated growth phase
   3. Stationary Phase
   4. Decline Phase
HANDLING FOODS SAFELY
   Storing Foods
   Cooling Foods Safely
   Reheating Foods

Holding Cooked Foods at Service Temperature
Thawing Foods
HAZARD ANALYSIS CRITICAL CONTROL POINT
(HACCP)
Sidebar *Identifying Critical Control Points*
Maintaining High Standards of Cleanliness
    The Role of the Uniform
Sidebar *A Germ-Free Uniform*
        The Hat
        The Jacket and Pants
        Apron and Side Towels
        Shoes
        Neckerchief
    Pest Control
    Cleaning and Sanitizing
        Ware Washing
SAFETY ISSUES
    Occupational Safety and Health (OSHA)
    Fire Safety
    Americans with Disabilities Act (ADA)
    A Special Note about Smokers
    Drugs and Alcohol in the Workplace
SUMMARY

Discussion Topics

TOPIC: Safety Issue Horror Stories:
• E coli outbreak in 1993 from Jack-in-the-Box hamburgers
    Confirmed cases: 583
    Hospitalization: 171
    Deaths: 4
(subsequent lawsuits against Jack-in-the-Box included case of 4-year-old girl with colon, kidney, and pancreas damage who received $5 million).
• Two hundred twenty four thousand people were infected with salmonella poisoning in 1994 when independent trucker hauled Schwan's ice cream mix in the same tanker that was used to haul raw eggs on alternate runs. (As a result of subsequent lawsuits, Schwan's Sales Enterprises, Inc. was required to pay between $80 and $75,000 to as many as 100,000 people).
• In 1994 forty people in Wisconsin got salmonella poisoning after eating raw ground beef

from a local butcher. State inspectors found that the employees had not properly cleaned the meat grinder.

TOPIC: Food Processing Plants and What Can Go Wrong
• Inspections and standards
• Mislabeling
• Recalls
• Ninety-three people contracted salmonella poisoning from beef jerky which had not been properly prepared at a local plant in New Mexico in 1995.

TOPIC: Mad cow disease
• Concerns over cows that came from England and are now part of herds in this country
• Even though meat is not imported, certain by-products are (tallow, gelatin, etc.)
• Impact on European and global markets

TOPIC: Hazard Analysis Critical Control Point (HACCP)
• What is it?
• Where to obtain info about it
• How and when to use it

Resource: Books

The HACCP Food Safety Manual. Joan K. Loken, CFE. John Wiley & Sons, Inc. New York, 1995.
The HACCP Reference Manual. National Restaurant Association. Chicago, 1993.
• USDA has established HACCP programs for seafood processors which must be instituted by 1998. It is estimated that these programs will eliminate up to 60,000 cases of seafood poisoning annually. (There are currently 114,000 cases of seafood poisoning each year in the United States.) Restaurateurs believe this will boost the public's confidence in seafood and therefore indirectly boost sales.

TOPIC: Drug and Alcohol Abuse

Resource: Video

Sanitation is Not an Option. *Culinary Institute of America,* 1992.

Resource: Book

Accident Prevention for Hotels, Motels, and Restaurants. Robert L. Kohr. Van Nostrand Reinhold. New York 1991.

Assignments

1 An office manager bought a cake from the local bakery for an office party. That evening all of the employees felt sick. The next day the office manager went to the bakery to report the incident. As the baker, how would you handle the situation?
   • Apology
   • Refund
   • Free offering
   • Incident report
   • Check remaining products
   • Determine cause to eliminate problem in the future
   • See also pages 39, 49–50

2 You are working as a sous chef in a seaside restaurant. During lunch service, the steam table goes out and the food reaches temperatures in the danger zone for over an hour. One of the cooks relights the steam table and says its not a problem because it has only been one hour, not three. What would you do?
   • Since three hours is the maximum total time food can be in the danger zone, it is better to take extra care and practice safe food handling:
      Any food that has been reheated once (food from a previous service) should probably be discarded
      Using a thermometer, test the temperature of all the food on the steam table
      Remove all foods with temperatures in the danger zone and reheat on the stove or in the oven before returning to the steam table
      Give a training session to your staff on safe food handling
      See also pages 44–45, 47, 45–50.

3 Chef Scungilli noticed that the fresh tuna was not moving as quickly as anticipated. He also noticed that the quality of the fish in the walk-in had been lessening and a noticeable odor had begun to eminate from the tuna. He instructed one of the cooks to rinse the fish with some lemon juice and put it on fresh ice. Chef Scungilli knows that bacteria can cause spoilage, but that you can kill the bacteria with a strong acidic substance like lemon juice. As expected, the fish lost the unpleasant odor and the tuna could easily pass as a quality menu item. Chef said it was important to keep food cost down, since times are finacially tough. What do you think of Chef's decision? Is there anything wrong with the facts that the chef has? Would you have done anything differently? Is there a better approach to using acids in this situation?
   • Lemon juice will not kill bacteria.
   • The fish should have been discarded.
   • When the fish was purchased it should have been placed on ice. The ice should have been changed daily.
   • If the chef had caught this in advance, he or she might have put the fish on special (or prepared a special appetizer) to have it move more quickly.
   • See also pages 43, 45.

4 A fire on the grill sets off the Ansel system an hour before service. Do you know what happens?
   • A fine white film will settle over the entire kitchen, working its way into the cracks. Most likely the kitchen will need to be closed and service delayed while the kitchen is cleaned.

5 A busload of senior citizens on a tour of a wine-growing region stops at a roadside diner. The special of the day is an egg salad platter with coleslaw and potato salad. Several of the tourists order it. Several hours later, some begin to complain of various symptoms. Eventually, two

men and a woman are hospitalized. What might have caused the problems?

- The mayonnaise in the salads might have been contaminated.
- The eggs may have been contaminated with salmonella.
- A worker with a cut on his or her hand may have tossed the salad with bare hands.
- See also pages 40–41, 43–45.

6 Cross-contamination is probably one of the most notorious forms of spreading foodborne illness. There are many situations where cross-contamination might occur in a normal working day. Name some of them, and outline how changing personal behavior and/or the organization of the workplace might help prevent cross-contamination from taking place.

   Situations, e.g.

- Using the same cutting board for meat and vegetables
- Using the slicer to slice meat, then cheese
- Not washing your hands at appropriate times
- Using your side towel to wipe your hands

   Solutions, e.g.:

- Properly train employees in safe food-handling practices
- Properly train staff on proper hygiene, if necessary
- Consider using color-coded cutting boards
- Have bleach and water buckets available at all stations (sanitizing solution and wiping cloths)
- Have cleaning supplies, sinks, and hand-washing sinks readily available
- See also pages 45, 50–52.

7 A worker with basically sound work habits has a slight allergy attack. He rubs his eyes, then begins preparing a rice pilaf. What should he have done?

- The employee should wash his hands carefully before preparing the pilaf.
- The empoyee should be trained on safe food handling.
- See also pages 42–43.

8 The kitchen is arranged so that the sink for handwashing is difficult to reach and is often out of soap. Suggest some remedies.

- Designate a different sink for handwashing.
- Move equipment or tables to make it easier to get to the handwashing sink.
- Designate someone to be in charge of keeping the handwashing sink stocked with anti-bacterial soap, nail brush, disposable towels, paper container.

9 In the middle of service, it is necessary to cut chicken breast into paillards, then slice cucumbers for garnish. What steps should be taken to assure that the line cook will be able to quickly and easily clean and sanitize the cutting board and the knife?

- The best solution is to have different cutting boards for chicken and vegetables.
- In either case, the cutting board and knife should be washed and then should be cleaned with a bleach/water solution.
- See also page 52.

Answer Key to Self-Study Questions

1 (a) Food safety: preparation and service of safe food in a clean environment by healthy food workers.
   (b) Sanitary, safe, and wholesome eating environment is important for the well-being of customers and employees—it will generate repeat customers and determine the success of the operation.

2 • Chemical
   • Physical
   • Biological

3 • Protein-rich
   • Moist
   • Have a moderate pH of between 4.6 and 10.

4 • Staphylococcus
   • Salmonellosis
   • Trichinosis
   • Botulism
   • Ergotism
   • Shigellosis

- Bacillus cereus
- Streptococcus
- Infectious hepatitis
- Perfringens

5
- Improper storage of foods
- Improper cooling of foods before storage
- Reheating foods improperly
- Holding cooked foods at inappropriate service temperatures
- Thawing foods improperly

6
- Wipe up spills immediately
- Let coworkers know that you are coming up behind them with something hot or sharp
- Alert the pot washer if pots, pans, and handles are especially hot
- Respect knives and handle them carefully
- Know what to do in case of fires
- Learn about first aid, including how to deal with cuts and burns
- Pick up anything on the floor that might trip the unwary
- Get help before lifting anything heavy and use your legs, not your back
- Learn to administer the Heimlich maneuver, CPR, and mouth-to-mouth resusitation

7 A time and temperature relationship at which potentially hazardous foods are held, allowing pathogens to thrive—40 to 140°F (4 to 60°C).

8 *Large batches of hot liquids:*
(1) Split large batches into two or more small stainless steel containers
(2) Place them in a cold water bath and stir until cooled to a temperature of at least 40°F (4°C)

Semi-solid foods:
(1) Spread/place in a thin/single layer on a sheet pan
(2) Place in a refrigerator to cool as quickly as possible

Solid foods:
(1) Cut into slices or chunks whenever possible to reduce the diameter of the food
(2) Cool it down under refrigeration as quickly as possible

9 Food infection—occurs when food containing living bacteria is ingested and the bacteria continue to thrive and reproduce in the human gastrointestinal tract, usually causing illness within 12–48 hours.

Food intoxication—true food poisoning; food containing toxins produced by pathogens is ingested. Once in the human body, the toxins act like a poison, generally striking within the first 12 hours.

10 Move items from the freezer to the refrigerator.
Alternatives:
- Place wrapped foods under a stream of cool running water
- Defrost in a microwave.

11 Hazard Analysis Critical Control Points (pronounced "hass-up")—a system for assessing each individual foodservice operation's potential risks and hazards associated with food handling and service, and establishing measures for minimizing or eliminating those risks as much as possible
- Key points in the HACCP system:
  (1) Assessment of hazards and risks
  (2) Determining the critical control points (CCPs)
  (3) Establishing critical limits (CLs)
  (4) Establishing procedures for monitoring CCPs
  (5) Establishing corrective action plans
  (6) Establishing a system for maintaining records
  (7) Developing a system to verify and record actions

12 (1) Sort
(2) Scrape
(3) Prerinse
(4) Wash in detergent and water at least 120°F (49°C)
(5) Rinse in hot water (130°F/54°C)
(6) Sanitize in 170°F (77°C) water or chemical solution
(7) Drain
(8) Store

13 • Keep screens on all doors and windows
  • Cover and regularly dispose of all garbage
  • Fill in any holes that may exist in the the foundation of the building
  • Clean the kitchen regularly
  • Check incoming deliveries for evidence of pests
  • Discretionary use of pest-control measures, such as traps and insecticides.
14 • Know where the fire department phone number is posted
  • Know where the fire extinguisher is located and how to use it
  • Know where all of the emergency exit areas from the building are
  • Know where to assemble once safely outside the building.

Keywords

Accelerated growth phase: The part of a pathogens life cycle in which the rate of reproduction and growth exceeds the death rate.

Acid: A substance having a sour or sharp flavor. Most foods are somewhat acidic. Foods generally referred to as "acids" include citrus juice, vinegar, and wine. A substance's degree of acidity is measured on the pH scale; acids have a pH of less than 7.

ADA (Americans with Disabilities Act): Legislation intended to assure equal access to public areas to those with disabilities. Includes building codes and other standards that must be adhered to in all new construction or remodeling.

Alkali (noun); **alkaline** (adj.): A substance that tests at higher than 7 on the pH scale. Alkalis are sometimes described as having a slightly soapy flavor. Olives and baking soda are some of the few alkaline foods.

Anaerobic bacteria: Bacteria that do not require oxygen to function.

Bacteria: Microscopic organisms. Some have beneficial properties, others can cause foodborne illnesses when contaminated foods are ingested.

Biological contamination: The infection or intoxication of foods with pathogens including the following: bacteria, yeast or fungus, virus, or parasites.

Chemical contamination: The adulteration of foods with various chemicals, including chemical poisons, herbicides, insecticides, and cleansers.

Contaminated foods: Foods that have become adulterated through physical, chemical, or biological means, rendering them unsafe for human consumption.

CPR (Cardio-Pulmonary Resuscitation): A means of reviving an individual whose heart has stopped beating. Individuals can be certified in CPR by authorized groups and organizations such as the American Red Cross.

Critical Control Points (CCPs): A part of HACCP standards indicating that foods must meet specific standards regarding storage, reheating, or service temperatures in order to prevent contamination.

Cross-contamination: The transference of disease-causing elements from one source to another through physical contact.

Danger zone: The temperature range from 45 to 140°F (7 to 60°C), the most favorable condition for rapid growth of many pathogens.

Decline phase: The stage at which a pathogen's death rate exceeds the rate of growth and reproduction.

FIFO (first in, first out): A fundamental storage principle based on stock rotation. Products are stored and used so the oldest product is always used first.

Fire safety: A comprehensive program put in place to assure that all individuals are free from hazards associated with fire, including prevention and reaction strategies to cover all situations.

Foodborne disease (or illness): An illness in humans caused by the consumption of an adulterated food product. In order for a food borne illness to be considered official, it must involve two or more people who have eaten the same food and it must be confirmed by health officials.

Foodborne infection: Illness caused by consuming foods contaminated with living pathogens.

Foodborne intoxication (or poisoning): Illness caused by consuming foods contaminated with poisons, including those toxins produced as a by-product of the life cycle of other pathogens.

GRAS (Generally Recognized as Safe): A set of standards indicating the point at which nonedible elements found in foods (often as the result of harvesting or processing) have reached levels deemed unsafe for humans to consume.

HACCP (Hazard Analysis Critical Control Point): A monitoring system used to track foods from the time that they are received until they are served to consumers to assure that they are free from contamination and foodborne illness by establishing standards and controls for time and temperature, as well as safe handling practices.

Heimlich maneuver: First aid for choking; the application of sudden, upward pressure on the upper abdomen to force a foreign object from the windpipe.

Lag phase: The point at which a pathogen's rate of growth and reproduction is equal to the rate of death.

Mouth-to-mouth resuscitation: The process by which an individual assists someone who has stopped breathing to start again, by breathing into the mouth and/or nasal passages in a rhythmic manner. Often used in conjunction with CPR.

OSHA (Occupational Safety and Health Administration): An agency dedicated to assuring that workers are provided a safe, hazard-free working environment.

Pathogen: A disease-causing microorganism.

Personal hygiene: Keeping one's person clean.

pH scale: A scale with values from 0 to 14 representing degree of acidity. A measurement of 7 is neutral, 0 is most acidic and 14 is most alkaline. Chemically, pH measures the concentration/activity of the element hydrogen.

Physical contamination: Adulterating foods by dropping foreign objects (hair, bandages, or other nonfood items) into foods during preparation or service.

Potentially hazardous foods: Foods that contain adequate amounts of protein, moisture, and an appropriate pH, enabling them to support the growth and reproduction of pathogens at a rate conducive to establishing foodborne illness in affected foods.

Salmonellosis: Disease caused by consuming foods infected with salmonella.

Sanitizing: Using moist heat or chemicals to kill pathogens.

Stationary phase: The point of a pathogen's life cycle in which rates of death and reproduction are equal.

Toxic poisoning: A condition brought about by consuming toxins, both naturally occurring (as found in mushrooms and rhubarb leaves) or those added to foods during growing, harvesting, processing, or preparation.

Toxins: Naturally occurring poisons, particularly those produced by the metabolic activity of living organisms, such as bacteria.

Trichinosis: Disease caused by consuming foods (especially pork) adulterated with the trichinella spiralis parasite.

Nutrition and Healthy Cooking

Objectives

- Explain what is meant by dietary goals and recommendations (pages 61–64)
- Describe the USDA's Food Guide Pyramid, as well as the Mediterranean and Vegetarian Pyramids (pages 61–64)
- Define and properly use the basic language of nutrition (pages 65–73)
- Discuss the different types of diets and special nutritional concerns for vegetarians (pages 64–65)
- List the major dietary vitamins and minerals (pages 72–75)
- Name the seven guidelines for nutritional cooking (pages 75–77)
- Explain how to put these guidelines into practice through recipe development, "healthy" plate compositions and purchasing for nutrition (pages 77–81)

Lecture Outline

DIETARY GOALS AND RECOMMENDATIONS
   The Lessons of Traditional Diets
   Vegetarianism
      Vegans
      Fruititarian
      Ovo-vegetarians
      Lacto/ovo-vegetarian
      Pesco-vegetarian
      Semi-vegetarian
      Alternivore (situational vegetarian)
   Dietary Supplements and "Nutraceuticals"
THE LANGUAGE OF NUTRITION
   Calories
      Empty Calories

Sidebar Determining Daily Calorie Needs
   Carbohydrates
      Complex Carbohydrates
      Simple Carbohydrates
      Refined Sugars
      Fiber
      Meeting Carbohydrate and Fiber Requirements
   Proteins
      Essential Amino Acids
      Plant-based Proteins
      Meeting Protein Requirements in a Typical Diet
   Fats and Oils
      Monounsaturated Fats
      Polyunsaturated Fats

Saturated Fats
Cholesterol
Maintaining Proper Levels of Fat and Cholesterol in the Diet
Vitamins and Minerals
Water-Soluble Vitamins
Beta-Carotene
Antioxidants
Fat-Soluble Vitamins
Major Minerals
Trace Minerals
Dietary Requirements for Vitamins and Minerals
Water: "The Forgotten Nutrient"

THE SEVEN GUIDELINES FOR NUTRITIONAL COOKING

1. Cook all foods with care to preserve their nutritional value, flavor, texture, and appeal.
2. Shift the emphasis on plates toward grains, legumes, vegetables and fruits as the "center of the plate."
3. Serve appropriate portions of foods; know what a standard serving for all foods is.
4. Select foods that help to achieve the nutritional goals and guidelines your guests are striving to meet.
5. Opt for monounsaturated cooking fats and oils whenever possible and reduce the use of saturated fats.
6. Use calorie dense foods (eggs, cream, butter, cheeses, and refined sugars) moderately.
7. Learn a variety of seasoning and flavoring techniques to help reduce a reliance on salt.

Sidebar Batch Cooking
Sidebar Center of the Plate

PUTTING NUTRITION GUIDELINES INTO PRACTICE
Developing Menu Items and Recipes
Sidebar Recipe Makeover
Identifying Healthy Cooking Techniques
Purchasing For Nutrition
Reading Labels for Nutritional Information
SUMMARY

Discussion Topics

TOPIC: Responsibilities of the chef regarding health/trends/needs:
- Knowledge—keeping up with current information
- Truth in menu/no false claims:
  The waiter poured coffee into the customer's cup. The customer asked "is that decaf?" The waiter said, "If that's what you wanted—then that's what it is."
- Offering choices/do not dictate
  Customers will eat what they want
- Flexibility in ordering: substitutions, no oil, sauce on the side
- Training the waitstaff to know the food

TOPIC: New/different/trendy diets that are perceived as "healthy"
- Mediterranean

Resource: Book

The Mediterranean Diet. Nancy Harmon Jenkins. Bantam Books. New York, 1994.

- Pacific Rim
- Vegetarian
  mutual   supplementation,   complementary proteins
- Spa cuisine

TOPIC: Endorsements by nutritional organizations and experts
- State, local, and national approval ratings for menu items
- AHA
- Dean Ornish
- Fit for Life
- Pritiken

TOPIC: Foods as pharmaceuticals
- Mega dosing
- Enhancing nutritional value (added vitamins and minerals)

- Food fortification (added after being stripped)
- Supplements: Foods that are engineered to have specific nutritional qualities may be "prescribed"

Resource: Video

Techniques of Healthy Cooking:
  Tape I—Bases and Sauces; 1993.
  Tape II—Cooking Methods; 1993.
  Tape III—Breakfast, Accompaniments, and Desserts, 1993. *Culinary Institute of America*

Resource: Magazines

Eating Well, including bimonthly features; "Fitness Report," "Nutrition News," and "Nutrition Sense"
University of California at Berkeley Wellness Letter

Assignments

1 A customer asks the waiter if the onion soup has any meat in it and is told that it does not. When she tastes the soup, she finds that it is made with a beef broth and she returns it. The soup has to be discarded. How can this be avoided in the future?
   - Better training for the waitstaff.
   - Encourage the waitstaff to ask questions in the kitchen, even during busy service time.
   - Make sure the staff understands the significance of the query.
   - Perhaps the waiter misunderstood the question. He should have explained that while there was no meat in the soup, it was prepared with a meat broth.
   - It is helpful to have a copy of the menu with all items explained in detail at the maitre d' station for the waitstaff's use.
   - The chef should explain all specials to the waitstaff in a preservice meeting.
   - See also pages 64–65.

2 The menu has an entrée selection that sounds appealing and healthy. A customer orders it, but is unhappy with what he receives. He feels he has not been given enough food for the money he has paid. What could be done to resolve this issue?
   - "Healthy" entrées often translates into smaller meat portions. The price should either be reduced or the plate should include heartier portions of "side" items. A selection of five or six different grains and vegetables (a wedge of polenta with rice, haricot vert and beets) would look appealing on the plate.
   - See also pages 73–78.

3 Using seven nutritional guidelines (Pages 73–77), discuss some ways in which a restaurant can gradually begin to incorporate the dietary guidelines and an overall awareness of nutritional cooking into a menu. List changes the customer might notice and those the customer may not be aware of:
   - Replace animal fat with olive oil.
   - Replace fats with ricotta cheese in some instances.
   - Use lowfat milk rather than whole milk whenever possible.
   - Use evaporated skim milk instead of cream for some sauces and soups.
   - Use buttermilk or chicken stock to emulsify a creamy dressing.
   - Reduce meat portion size and add more grains and vegetables.
   - Offer fresh tomato sauces and vegetable purées as alternatives to cream-based sauces.
   - Use whole grains whenever possible.
   - Offer fresh fruit as a dessert choice.
   - See also pages 78–81.

4 The customer would like a lowfat entree. How could you convey that little fat was used in the preparation of a menu item without the customer needing to ask?
   Possibilities:
   - Description of how the item is prepared: "A dry rub is applied to the steak before it is grilled."

- Provide a key on menu which indicates low-fat items (in the same manner that spicy food is often noted).
- Be blunt: "No oil was used in the preparation of this dish."
- See also pages 79, 80.

5 Discuss alcohol consumption and its effect on the body. (What is considered moderation, how does the body assimilate alcohol, overall health benefits/dangers, etc.)
- Moderation: one or two glasses a day
- French paradox
- Differences in the way men's and women's bodies assimilate alcohol
- Aging process
- See also pages 63, 66–67.

6 What is metabolism? Is it true that some people's metabolism operates at a higher rate than others? Is there anything that can be done (positive/negative) to change one's metabolic rate?
- "The chemical changes in living cells by which energy is provided for vital processes and activities and new material is assimilated." (Webster's Ninth New Collegiate Dictionary, F. Mish, ed. Merriam-Webster, Inc., 1983.)
- Metabolism varies from individual to individual, affected by body weight and composition (lean muscle vs. fat), gender, age, and activity level.
- It is possible to increase metabolism by increasing muscle mass, weight loss, and/or increase in activity level.
- See also pages 65–66.

Answer Key to Self-Study Questions

1 (a) Nutrition—the study of the way humans make use of the foods they eat in order to fulfill the body's needs for growth, repair, and maintenance.
Healthy cooking—the ways that chef or restaurant owner can meet guests' needs for dishes that fit within specific nutritional guidelines.

(b) Restaurant patrons are
- increasingly asking for menu options that are lower in fats and/or cholesterol (sauce on side).
- more knowledgable regarding nutrition.

2 (a) Grains and starchy vegetables, including pasta, rice, cereals, breads, and other foods made from grains.
(b) fats, oils, and sweets.

3 • couscous
- bulgur
- quinoa
- kasha
- barley
- hominy
- millet
- oat groats
- wheat berries

4. Today's chef must understand how balanced nutrition can be achieved without animal products, and develop skill in properly preparing a variety of appealing vegetarian items. In addition to the rising number of vegetarians, there are many health-conscious people who occasionally select meatless or red-meatless meals when they dine out.

5 30 percent or less.

6 It contains all of the essential amino acids.

7 (a) Saturated fat.
(b) butter, well-marbled meats, lard, chicken skin, bacon, sausages, eggs, and tropical oils such as coconut and palm oil.

8 No. Only animal products contain cholesterol. Both animal products and nonanimal products can contain saturated fats.

9 (a) Fat-soluble—stored in fat tissues in the body and can reach toxic levels if ingested in great quantities. Include vitamins A, D, E, and K. These vitamins hold up fairly well in foods that contain them during cooking.
(b) Water-soluble—not stored in the body and need to be replenished daily. Includes vitamin C and the B vitamins. These vitamins are highly sensitive to heat, air, and light, and are easily destroyed.

10 (1) Calcium—milk, dairy products, canned salmon with bones

(2) Phosphorus—milk, poultry, fish, meats, cheese, nuts, cereals, legumes

(3) Sodium—salt, some canned foods, salt-cured meats, pickles

(4) Potassium—meats, cereals, vegetables, legumes, fruits

(5) Iron (trace mineral)—liver, meat, whole or enriched grains, green vegetables

11 (1) Cook all foods with care to preserve their nutritional value, flavor, texture, and appeal.

(2) Shift the emphasis on plates toward grains, legumes, vegetables, and fruits as the center of the plate.

(3) Serve standard serving-size portions of foods.

(4) Select foods that help to achieve the nutritional goals and guidelines your guests are striving to meet.

(5) Opt for monounsaturated cooking fats and oils whenever possible and reduce the use of saturated fats.

(6) Use calorie-dense foods (eggs, cream, butter, cheese, and refined sugars) moderately.

(7) Learn a variety of seasoning and flavoring techniques to help reduce reliance on salt.

12 (1) Couscous: ½ cup (although couscous is technically a pasta, it is usually treated as a grain)

(2) Grilled vegetables: ½ cup

(3) Seared salmon: 4–6 ounces.

Keywords

Acid/Base balance: A neutral state; "7" on the pH scale.

Alternivore: An individual who, while not a strict vegetarian, often prefers to order a meatless option from the menu.

Antioxidants: Noncaloric nutrients (vitamins, minerals, and enzymes) capable of attaching themselves to free radicals. This has the effect of preventing free radicals from damaging healthy cells.

Atherosclerosis: Condition caused by plaque build-up in the arteries.

Beta-carotene: A noncaloric nutrient found predominantly in fruits and vegetables such as carrots, squashes, leafy greens, and cabbages; a vitamin A precursor, associated with a healthful diet and possibly a decreased chance of developing various illness, such as cancer or cardio-vascular disease.

Batch cooking: The practice of preparing or reheating foods in smaller batches to maximize nutrient retention and minimize loss through waste.

Calorie: A unit used to measure food energy. It is the amount of energy needed to raise the temperature of 1 gram of water by 1°C.

Carbohydrate: One of the basic nutrients used by the body as a source of energy.

Center of the plate: An expression meant to focus attention on the food item that provides the primary culinary and nutritional focus. Center of the plate first came to public attention when various eating plans and pyramids suggested moving meat away from its position as "center of the plate."

Complete proteins: Foods that contain all the essential amino acids (those amino acids that cannot be produced in the body). Animal foods are considered complete proteins.

Complex carbohydrate: A large molecule made up of long chains of sugar molecules. In food, these molecules are found in starches and fiber.

Dietary cholesterol: Cholesterol which is consumed in foods.

Dietary supplement: A formulation (pill, powder, liquid) taken as an adjunct to foods consumed throughout the day.

Empty calories: Calories derived from foods that have been refined or stripped of other nutrients.

Essential amino acids: Protein components that cannot be produced in the diet and which must be obtained from a dietary source.

Fat-soluble vitamins: Vitamins (specifically A, D, E) that are dissolved and stored in fat, both in foods and in the body. Relatively stable during moist-heat cooking methods.

Fat: One of the basic nutrients used by the body to provide energy. Fats also provide flavor in food and give a feeling of fullness.

Fiber: The structural component of plants that is necessary to the human diet. Sometimes referred to as roughage.

Fructose: Fruit sugar, occurs naturally in fruits; may also be refined.

Fruitarian: An individual who consumes no meat products, heavy emphasis on fresh fruits.

Glucose: Simple sugar; body's preferred source of energy.

High-density lipoproteins (HDL): A type of fatty acid often referred to as "good cholesterol" due to its role in helping to flush the arteries of plaque that could otherwise build up on the lining of the artery wall, leading to atherosclerosis.

Hypertension: High blood pressure; typically caused by a constriction of the blood vessels due to a mineral imbalance (too much sodium, e.g.) tension, or stress.

Lactose: The simple sugar found in milk.

Lacto/Ovo-vegetarian: An individual that eats a predominantly meatless diet, plus eggs and dairy foods.

Low-density lipo-proteins (LDL): A substance related to cholesterol, typically associated with such conditions as atherosclerosis and cardio-vascular disease. High levels of LDL in the blood indicate an increased likelihood of fatty deposits known as plaque building up in arteries.

Maltose: A disaccharide made from 2 molecules of glucose.

Mediterranean Food Pyramid: A graphic representation of the optimal healthy diet of the Mediterranean region, developed by the World Health Organization (WHO) and Oldway's Exchange and Preservation Trust.

Monounsaturated fat: A fat with one available bonding site not filled with a hydrogen atom. Food sources include avocado, olives, and nuts.

Nutrients: The basic components of foods used by the body for growth, repair, restoration, and energy: carbohydrates, fats, proteins, water, vitamins, and minerals.

Nutrition: The processes by which an organism takes in and uses food.

Oils: Substance extracted from vegetables, nuts, and seeds; a cooking fat that is pourable at room temperature.

Ovo-vegetarian: A person whose diet consists of plant-based foods, with the addition of eggs.

Pesco-vegetarian: A person who consumes a diet based primarily on plant-based foods with the addition of eggs, dairy, and fish.

Polyunsaturated fat: A fat with more than one available bonding site not filled with a hydrogen atom. Food sources include corn, cottonseed, safflower, soy, and sunflower oils.

Protein: One of the basic nutrients needed by the body to maintain life, supply energy, build and repair tissues, form enzymes and hormones, and perform other essential functions. Protein can be obtained from animal and vegetable sources.

Refined sugar: A simple carbohydrate that has been processed to remove all additional elements and separate it from its original source; table sugar, honey, corn syrup, and molasses are examples.

Saturated fat: A fat whose available bonding sites are entirely filled with hydrogen atoms. These tend to be solid at room temperature and are primarily of animal origin. (Coconut and palm oil are vegetable sources of saturated fat.) Food sources include butter, meat, cheese, chocolate, and eggs.

Semi-vegetarian: An individual who occasionally follows a meatless eating plan.

Serum cholesterol: A measure of the cholesterol found in an individual's blood.

Simple carbohydrate: Any of a number of small carbohydrate molecules (mono-and disaccharides), including fructose, lactose, maltose, and sucrose.

Situational vegetarian: An individual who may opt for meatless meal option when available.

Standard serving (or portion) sizes: Serving sizes based on calorie and nutrient requirements.

Trace minerals: Nutritive, but noncaloric, elements necessary in the diet, measure in very small units. In some cases, dietary requirements may not yet have been determined.

Tropical oils: Oils derived from tropical plants such as coconut, palm, and palm kernel.

USDA Food Guide Pyramid: A graphic representation of an optimal diet, based on several tiers. The foundation of this diet includes whole grains (breads, pasta, rice, etc.). The smaller the tier, the fewer portions should be consumed on a daily basis.

USRDA: The suggested minimum requirements for various nutrients, necessary to prevent the onset of deficiency diseases.

Vegan: An individual who follows a strictly meatless diet, excluding all animal products.

Vegetarian: An individual whose diet is primarily plant based; there are different forms of vegetarian diets including vegan, fruititarian, ovo-and lacto/ovo-vegetarian, pesco-vegetarian, and semi-vegetarian.

Vegetarian Pyramid: A graphic representation of the optimal vegetarian diet.

Water-soluble vitamins: Vitamin C and B that can dissolve in water and are therefore easily excreted from the body and are also susceptible to loss during cooking in water.

CHAPTER 4

Equipment Identification

Objectives

- Understand the rules for knife care, use, and storage (pages 86–88)
- Identify the different parts of a knife (pages 88–90)
- Understand the differences in knife construction and quality (pages 88–90)
- Describe a variety of sharpening and honing tools and their function (pages 91–92)
- Name a variety of hand tools and their uses (page 92)
- Identify some of the most frequently used pieces of small equipment (pages 93–94)
- Learn the basic rules for working safely with large and small equipment (interspersed, pages 93-100)
- Identify pots and pans, their composition, purpose, and appropriate care (pages 94–97)
- Identify the equipment used in several categories of work, including:
    Slicing, grinding, and grating (pages 98–99)
    Mixing and puréeing (pages 98–99)
    Cooking: stovetops, ovens, grills, fryers, steamers, kettles (pages 100–102)
    Refrigeration and freezing (page 102)

Lecture Outline

KNIVES
1. Handle knives with respect.
2. Keep knives sharp.
3. Keep knives clean.
4. Use safe handling procedures for knives.
5. Use an appropriate cutting surface.
6. Keep knives properly stored.

THE PARTS OF A KNIFE
   Blades
   Tangs
   Handles
   Rivets
   Bolsters

TYPES OF KNIVES
   Chef's Knife, or French Knife
   Utility Knife
   Paring Knife
   Boning Knife
   Filleting Knife
   Slicer
   Cleaver
   Tourné Knife

SHARPENING AND HONING TOOLS
  Sharpening Stones
    Carborundum Stones
    Arkansas Stones
    Diamond-impregnated Stones
  Steels
HAND TOOLS
  Rotary Swivel-Bladed Peeler
  Parisienne Scoop (Melon Baller)
  Kitchen Fork
  Palette Knife (Metal Spatula)
  Whips
  Offset Spatula
  Pastry Bag
SMALL EQUIPMENT
  Measuring Equipment
    Graduated Measuring Pitchers and Cups
    Scales
    Thermometers
    Measuring Spoons
  Bowls for Mixing
  Storage Containers
  Sieves, Strainers, and Chinois
    Food Mill
    Drum Sieve (Tamis)
    Chinois
    Colander
    Ricer
    Cheesecloth
POTS, PANS, AND MOLDS
  Copper
  Cast Iron
  Stainless Steel
  Blue-Steel, Black-Steel, Pressed-Steel, or Rolled-Steel Pans
  Sidebar Proper Care and Cleaning of Copper Pans
  Aluminum
  Nonstick Coatings

The following guidelines should be observed when choosing a pan or mold:

• Choose a size appropriate to the food being cooked.
• Choose material appropriate to the cooking technique.

• Use proper handling, cleaning, and storing techniques.
• Be sure to dry pans before storing
Sidebar Seasoning Pans
  Pots and Pans for Stove Top Cooking
    Stockpot (Marmite)
    Saucepot
    Saucepan
    Rondeau
    Sauteuse
    Sautoir
    Omelet Pan/Crêpe Pan
    Bain-Marie (Double Boiler)
    Griddle
    Fish Poacher
    Steamer
    Specialty Pots And Pans: Woks, Couscousières, Paella Pans, and Grill Pans
  Pots and Pans for Oven Cooking
    Roasting Pan
    Sheet Pan
    Hotel Pan
    Pâté Mold
    Terrine Mold
    Gratin Dish
    Soufflé Dish
    Timbale Mold
    Specialty Molds

LARGE EQUIPMENT
  Safety Precautions
    1. Obtain proper instruction in the machine's safe operation. Do not be afraid to ask for extra help.
    2. First turn off and then unplug electrical equipment before assembling or breaking down the equipment.
    3. Use all safety features: Be sure that lids are secure, hand guards are used, and the machine is stable.
    4. Clean and sanitize the equipment thoroughly after each use.
    5. Be sure that all pieces of equipment are properly reassembled and left unplugged after each use.

6. Report any problems or malfunctions promptly and alert coworkers to the problem.

    Grinding, Slicing, and Puréeing Equipment
      Meat Grinder
      Vertical Chopping Machine (VCM)
      Food Chopper (Buffalo Chopper)
      Food Processor
      Food/Meat Slicer
      Mandoline
    Kettles and Steamers
      Steam-Jacketed Kettle
      Tilting Kettle
      Pressure Steamer
      Convection Steamer
STOVES, RANGES, AND OVENS
    Ranges
      Open Burner
      Flat-Top
      Ring-Top
      Induction Burner
    Ovens
      Convection Oven
      Conventional/Deck Ovens
      Slow Cookers/Combi Stoves
      Smokers
Sidebar Tandoori Oven
    Griddles and Grills
      Griddle
      Grills, Broilers, Salamander
REFRIGERATION EQUIPMENT
    Walk-In
    Reach-In
    On-Site Refrigeration
    Portable Refrigeration
    Display Refrigeration
    Ice Cream Freezer
SUMMARY

Discussion Topics

TOPIC: Latest equipment/design

Resource: Magazine

Food Arts, "Equipment" and "Table Top," monthly features
Chef, "Product Gallery," monthly feature

TOPIC: Restaurant providing equipment vs. employees using personal equipment.

TOPIC: Selecting equipment for a new kitchen.

TOPIC: Contemporary designers:
- Joe Baum, New York, NY (Windows on the World, Rainbow Room)
- Barbara Lazaroff, Los Angeles, CA (Spagos, Chinois on Main)
- Gilles Depardon, Kathryn Ogawa, Janis Leonard, New York, NY
- Ilan Waisbrod, Tenafly, NJ
- Wayne Turett, Stuart Basseches, New York, NY

Resource: Video

Knife Care: Selection, Sanitation and Safety. *Culinary Institute of America*, 1995.

Additional material for this chapter may be found in the back of this manual. See "Broilers and Grills."

Assignments

1   Most of the time, injuries in the kitchen are the result of carelessness while operating and cleaning equipment. When the prep cook began to clean the slicer, he cut his hand severely. What might have caused this?
- Carelessness.
- The machine was not turned off.
- The machine was not unplugged.
- The hand guard had been removed.
- See also page 99.

2   The oyster bar chef, who usually opens the oysters, is late for work. One of the prep cooks takes over but he can't find the oyster knife,

which the chef hides every evening so it doesn't disappear. Using his paring knife, the cook begins to serve the customers. Suddenly the tip of the knife breaks off and nicks the hand of the cook. The cook must leave the line. Name some problems with this situation and offer solutions:

- When individuals hide equipment, the restaurant must either purchase extra equipment, or other staff is required to use equipment not suited for the job.
- The paring knife should not have been used to open oysters.
- The cook should have been wearing a wire mesh glove which might have protected his hand.
- See also pages 86–88, 90–91, 287.

3 As the cooks do their daily prep, they consistently find they do not have enough bowls. When the day chef begins the inventory, she finds that all of the leftovers from the night before have been stored in stainless steel mixing bowls. How can this situation be avoided?

- Everyone should be instructed to use proper storage containers when putting away food. Mixing bowls use an unnecessary amount of space in the walk-in and storage area. The day crew will now have to transfer the food and will lose a lot of time.
- Name some appropriate storage containers according to food item and storage time.
- See also page 93.

4 The pastry chef is preparing lemon curd. As she mixes the curd in the saucepan, it gets a grayish hue. When she tastes the curd, it has a slightly metallic taste. How did this happen and what should be done?

- Probably an aluminum pan was used to mix the lemon curd.
- Discard batch and make a fresh one.
- See also pages 94–95.

5 Proper respect for one's tools is the hallmark of a chef's professionalism. What are some ways that a kitchen can be organized to make sure that equipment is handled carefully,

safely, and efficiently to get the best possible results?

- Appropriate racks and drawers for specific tools.
- Separate rack or drawer for knives.
- No knives or sharp tools left in dish sink.
- No hot pots and pans left in dish sink or by sink (without warning).
- Dishwasher puts away all equipment immediately after it dries.
- Only trained individuals allowed to use equipment.
- See also pages 86–88.

6 Why is a sharp knife a safer knife to work with than a dull one?

- Sharp knives require less pressure as you cut than dull ones.
- A dull knife is more likely to slip on the surface of whatever it is cutting. A sharp knife will slice through.
- If you cut yourself, a dull knife will make a worse cut.
- See also pages 86, 91–92.

7 Discuss the importance of respecting ownership of equipment, for both the restaurant and employees' personal equipment.

- Never use anyone's personal equipment without permission.
- Always return the equipment in the same condition or better than it was received.
- Never use a tool for a job that it was not intended for.
- See also Question 2 above.
- See also page 86.

Answer Key to Self-Study Questions

1 (a) It is an all-purpose knife used for most chopping, slicing, and mincing chores and is the most important tool a chef will ever have.

   (b) It is an extension of your hand—select the one which will fit your hand the best. A good-quality knife, if properly cared for, can last a lifetime.

2 • Carbon steel
• Stainless steel
• High-carbon stainless steel.

3 (a) • Construction
• Sharpness
• Longevity of the blades.

(b) Taper-ground blades are forged from one sheet of metal, they are harder to keep sharp, but they tend to be longer lasting. Hollow-ground blades are forged from two sheets of metal with beveled or fluted edges, which tend to hold a sharp edge better, but are less durable.

4 Full tang—visibly runs the length of the entire handle and is the most durable
• Partial tang—runs only part way down the length of the handle and is less durable
• Rat-tail tang—thin pieces of metal that are completely encased in the handle, and generally do not hold up well.

5 • Handle the knife with respect
• Keep it sharp with frequent honing with a steel and the occasional use of a sharpening stone
• Keep it clean
• Use safe handling procedures
• Use an appropriate cutting surface
• Properly store it

6 (1) Assess how dull it is—if the knife is severely dulled, it may be necessary to have it professionally reground on a grinding wheel or electric sharpener.

(2) Sharpen with a stone
• Follow a consistent pattern of usage: either dry, with water, or with oil
• Begin with the coarsest stone surface and move to the finest
• Apply the proper motion, correct angle, and even pressure to be most effective

(3) Hone with a steel, at correct angle, with even pressure

(4) Maintain blade between sharpenings by honing with a steel

7 • Steel
• Glass
• Ceramic
• Diamond-impregnated surfaces

8 (1) Cutting up a chicken—boning knife and a cleaver or chef's knife (depending on the size of the bird and the thickness of bone)

(2) Peeling carrots—rotary or swivel-blade peeler

(3) Making whipped egg whites or heavy cream—balloon whip and a bowl (ideally copper)

(4) puréeing strawberries—food processor, blender, immersion blender

9 *Volume:*
• Milk
• Eggs
• Juice
• Oil
• Most liquid items
• Some portioned servings (2 fluid ounces sauce, ½ cup rice)
• Some prepped vegetables

Weight:
• Flour
• Sugar
• Vegetables
• Meat
• Solid chocolate
• Solid butter
• Most solid items
• Some portioned servings (6 ounces steak)

10 • Colander
• Fine chinois
• Cheesecloth

11 *Material*	*Advantages*	*Disadvantages*
• Stainless steel	easy maintenance, will not react with food	only moderately good conductor of heat
• Copper	transfers heat rapidly and evenly	might affect color and consistency of food
• Cast iron	holds and transmits heat effectively and evenly	brittle, rusts and scars easily
• Blue-steel	transmits heat rapidly	prone to discoloration
• Black-steel	transmits heat rapidly	prone to discoloration
• Pressed-steel	transmits heat rapidly	prone to discoloration
• Rolled-steel	transmits heat rapidly	prone to discoloration
• Aluminum	excellent conductor of heat	soft metals, wears quickly, may affect color of food
• Variety of nonstick coatings	foods require less fats and oils	fragile, delicate

Special care for copper—mix equal parts flour and salt; add vinegar to make a paste. Coat copper with paste and clean.

12 • If the pot is too large, a sauce made from the cuisson will lack flavor intensity and it is easy to overcook the fish.
  • If the pot is too small, there may not be enough cuisson available to make a sauce.

13 *Benefits*
  • Transfers heat rapidly
  • Reacts especially well with egg whites for whipping
  Disadvantages
  • Requires great care and labor to keep clean
  • Cooking surfaces need to be retinned regularly

14 • Helps to prevent chips, dents, and breakage.
  • Makes it easier to find and get to the specific pieces of cookware needed at any given time during the day.

15 *Deck ovens:*
  • Ideal for roasting foods
  • Provide stable, easy-to-clean cooking surfaces with no wire racks
  • Heat emanates from below
  • Operate efficiently on gas or electric energy
  Convection ovens:
  • Cook food evenly and quickly
  • Are often able to introduce moisture into the oven cavity as well

Slow cookers
  • Cook at low temperatures
  • May also be used to steam foods
  • Good for holding foods at service temperature

Keywords

Aluminum: A metal commonly used for various cooking vessels; relatively soft.

Arkansas stone: A special stone used to sharpen knifes.

Bain-Marie: A water bath used to cook foods gently by surrounding the cooking vessel with simmering water. Also, a set of nesting pots with single, long handles used as a double boiler. Also, steam table inserts.

Black steel: A type of rolled or pressed steel used to make sauté pans, omelet and crêpe pans, as well as baking pans.

Blade: The portion of a knife that is used for cutting, slicing, and chopping.

Blue steel: See black steel.

Bolster: A collar or shank at the point on a knife where the blade meets the handle.

Boning knife: A thin-bladed knife used for separating raw meat from the bone; its blade is usually about six inches long.

Broiler: The piece of equipment used to broil foods. Heat source is located above foods, cooking them via radiant heat.

Candy stove/stockpot range: A small, free-standing single-burner range with a series of rings, typically used to hold a single pot, such as a candy pot or stockpot.

Carbon steel: A blend of carbon and stainless steel commonly used to manufacture knife blades.

Carborundum stone: A sharpening stone; available in various "grits" to sharpen knives to the desired degree of fineness.

Cast iron: Iron, heated and poured into molds, used to make a variety of pots and pans.

Chafing dish: A metal dish with a heating unit (flame or electric) used to keep foods warm and to cook foods at the table side or during buffet service.

Cheesecloth: A light, fine mesh gauze used for straining liquids and making sachets.

Chef's or French knife: An all-purpose knife used for chopping, slicing, and mincing; its blade is usually between eight and 14 inches long.

Chinois: A conical sieve used for straining and puréeing foods.

Cleaver: A cutting tool with a large heavy blade; available in a range of sizes. Chinese cleavers are typically sharpened on one side of the blade. Butcher's cleavers are heavy enough to cut through bones and joints.

Colander: A perforated bowl, with or without a base or legs, used to strain foods.

Convection oven: An oven that employs convection currents by forcing hot air through fans so it circulates around food, cooking it quickly and evenly.

Convection steamer: Steamer unit in which steam is generated in a separate chamber and vented over the foods.

Conventional oven: Enclosed chamber, usually with adjustable racks used to cook foods. Air is heated by means of heating elements located under the floor of the oven.

Copper: A metal favored for used in pots, pans, and bowls. Typically lined with aluminum, tin, or steel for most applications, copper bowls and preserving pans are often left unlined. Foods should never be allowed to remain in contact with copper for extended periods to avoid chance of toxic poisoning.

Couscoussière: Special nested pots used to prepare couscous and its accompanying stew.

Deck oven: A variant of the conventional oven, in which the heat source is located underneath the deck or floor of the oven and the food is placed directly on the deck instead of on a rack.

Diamond-impregnated stone: A sharpening or honing tool that has been produced with industrial-grade diamonds over the surface. Felt by many chefs to offer superior sharpening abilities.

Die: The plate in a meat grinder through which foods pass, just before a blade cuts them. The size of the die's opening determines the fineness of the grind.

Drum sieve (tamis): A sieve consisting of a screen stretched across a shallow cylinder of wood or aluminum.

Feed tray: a holding tray directly on the grinder where foods to be ground can be placed.

Filleting knife: A flexible-bladed knife used for filleting fish; similar in size and shape to a boning knife.

Fish poacher: A long, narrow pot with straight sides and possibly a perforated rack, used for poaching whole fish.

Flat-top range: A thick plate of cast iron or steel set over the heat source on a range; diffuses heat, making it more even than an open burner.

Food chopper (Buffalo chopper): A piece of cutting equipment that holds foods in a rotating bowl; blades are housed in the machine.

Food mill: A type of strainer with a crank-operated, curved blade. It is used to purée soft foods.

Food processor: A machine with interchangeable blades and disks and a removable bowl and lid separate from the motor housing. It can be used for a variety of tasks, including chopping, grinding, puréeing, emulsifying, kneading, slicing, shredding, and cutting julienne.

Food/meat slicer: A machine that has a rotating circular blade and a carrier, used to slice meats and other foods very thinly. May be motorized.

Full tang: A blade constructed so that a section of the blade extends the entire length and width of the handle.

Graduated measuring pitchers and cups: Utensils used to measure liquid and volume of ingredients.

Gratin dish: A cooking vessel used to hold foods that are to be browned under the broiler or salamander.

Griddle: A heavy metal surface, which may be either fitted with handles, built into a stove, or heated by its own gas or electric element. Cooking is done directly on the griddle.

Grill pan: A skillet with ridges that is used to simulate grilling on the stove top.

Grill; grilling: A cooking technique in which foods are cooked by a radiant heat source placed below the food. Also, the piece of equipment on which grilling is done. Grills may be fueled by gas, electricity, charcoal, or wood.

Griswold: A cast iron cooking pan.

Grit: Degree of fineness or coarseness of a sharpening stone.

Hand guard: A carrier or other protective device found on cutting and slicing equipment, intended to protect the hands from accidental injury.

High-carbon stainless steel: A blend of steel and carbon used to make knife blades.

Hollow-ground: A type of knife blade made by fusing two sheets of metal and beveling or fluting the edge.

Hotel pan: A rectangular metal pan, in any of a number of standard sizes, with a lip that allows it to rest in a storage shelf or steam table.

Ice cream freezer: A utensil used to simultaneously churn and cool a base in order to produce frozen items such as ice cream or sherbet.

Induction burner: A type of heating unit that relies on magnetic attraction between the cook top and metals in the pot to generate the heat that cooks foods in the pan. Reaction time is significantly faster than with traditional burners.

Kitchen fork: A hand tool used to stabilize foods that are being sliced or carved, to turn foods, or to test for doneness (fork tender).

Mandoline: A slicing and cutting tool, named for the stroking motion used as foods are passed over the blades.

Measuring spoons: A set of spoons of standard sizes, used to measure tablespoons, teaspoons, and fractions of teaspoons.

Meat grinder: A piece of equipment used to process meat by feeding meat cubes or strips through a tube, cutting the meat as it passes through a die plate.

Nonstick coating: A special finish applied to the interior of cooking and baking pans to reduce the need for adding oils and shortenings to prepare the pan.

Offset spatula: A hand tool with a wide, bent blade set in a short handle, used to turn or lift foods from grills, broilers, or griddles.

Omelet pan/crêpe pan: A pan used to prepare omelets or crêpes.

On-site refrigeration: Refrigerators or refrigerated drawers located on the cooking line to hold service mise en place.

Open-burner range: A type of cooking range in which a heat source is allowed direct contact with the pan.

Paella pan: A specialized pan for cooking paella; it is wide and shallow and usually has two loop handles.

Palette knife: A flexible, round-tipped knife used to turn pancakes and grilled foods and to spread fillings and glazes; may have a serrated edge. (Also called a metal spatula.)

Paring knife: A short knife used for paring and trimming fruits and vegetables; its blade is usually two to four inches long.

Parisienne scoop (melon baller): A small tool used for scooping balls out of vegetable or fruit.

Partial tang: The portion of the knife blade that extends into the handle; does not extend full length of the handle.

Pastry bag and tips: A bag—usually made of plastic, canvas, or nylon—that can be fitted with plain or decorative tips and used to pipe out icings and puréed foods.

Pâté mold: A hinged loaf pan used to prepare pâté en croûte.

Portable refrigeration: Cold food storage cabinets or carts with wheels or casters, enabling easy repositioning to suit kitchen needs.

Pressed steel: A type of metal used to construct various cooking pans, especially crêpe and omelet pans.

Pressure steamer: A type of steam unit that generates steam under pressure in the cooking cavity.

Pusher: A wooden or plastic plunger used to move foods into the feed tube of a meat grinder.

Range: A term used to describe a cooking surface. Often, an oven unit is part of a range's configuration.

Rat-tail tang: A very thin rod, extending from the handle into the blade of a knife.

Reach-in refrigeration: A refrigeration unit, or set of units, with pass-through doors. They are often used in the pantry area for storage of salads, cold hors d'oeuvre, and other frequently used items.

Ricer: A hand tool used to purée cooked potatoes and similar foods; the food is loaded into a hopper and a metal plate is used to press the soft food through the holes in the hopper.

Ring-top range: A flat-top with removable plates that can be opened to varying degrees to expose more or less direct heat.

Rivets: Bolts used to secure the handle to the tang.

Roasting pan: A shallow pan, with or without a cover, used to roast foods. Available in a range of sizes and materials.

Rolled steel: A type of metal used to construct various cooking pans, especially woks.

Rondeau: A shallow, wide, straight-sided pot with two loop handles.

Rotary peeler: A vegetable peeler with a swivel blade.

Salamander: See Broiler.

Saucepan: A pot used for stovetop cooking; typically has a single handle and is taller than it is wide.

Saucepot: Similar to a saucepan, but often has two loop handles.

Sauteuse: A shallow skillet with sloping sides and a single, long handle. Used for sautéing and referred to generically as a sauté pan.

Sautoir: A shallow skillet with straight sides and a single, long handle. Used for sautéing and referred to generically as a sauté pan.

Scales: Measuring tools used to determine weight.

Seasoning: (1) The process by which a cast iron or steel pan is treated to create a surface seal.
(2) The process of adjusting the final flavor of a dish.

Sharpening stone: A stone used to restore the edge of a dull knife.

Sheet pan: A flat baking pan, often with a rolled lip, used to cook foods in the oven.

Slicer: A tool made with a rotating circular blade and a carriage to hold foods. Foods are cut thinly as the blade turns against the food.

Slow cooker/combi stove: A piece of cooking equipment that prepares foods at a very low, even temperature. Some units can also steam foods and/or hold them for service.

Smoker: An enclosed area in which foods are held on racks or hooks and allowed to remain in a smoke bath at the appropriate temperature.

Soufflé dish: A ceramic, porcelain, or metal dish with straight, smooth sides used to prepare sweet or savory soufflés.

Stainless steel: A metal alloy used to construct various pieces of cookware; does not discolor, stain, pit or rust in the presence of acids, heat, or water.

Steam-jacketed kettle: A kettle with double-layered walls, between which steam circulates, providing even heat for cooking stocks, soups, and sauces. These kettles may be insulated, spigoted, and/or tilting. (The latter are also called trunnion kettles).

Steamer: A set of stacked pots with perforations in the bottom of each pot. They fit over a larger pot that is filled with boiling or simmering water. Also, a perforated insert made of metal or bamboo that can be inserted in a pot and used to steam foods.

Steel: A tool used to hone knife blades. It is usually made of steel but may be ceramic, glass, or diamond-impregnated metal.

Stockpot (marmite): A large, straight-sided pot that is taller than it is wide. Used for making stocks and soups. Some have spigots. (Also called a marmite).

Tang: The continuation of the knife blade into its handle. A full tang extends through the entire handle. A partial tang only runs through part of the knife. A rat-tail tang is thinner than the blade's spine and is encased in the handle and is not visible at the top or bottom edge.

Taper-ground: A type of knife blade forged out of a single sheet of metal, then ground so it tapers smoothly to the cutting edge. Taper-ground knives are generally the most desirable.

Terrine mold: The baking dish used to prepare terrines.

Thermometer: A tool used to measure internal or external temperatures.

Tilting kettle (Swiss kettle): A large, relatively shallow, tilting pot used for braising, stewing, and, occasionally, steaming.

Timbale/timbale mold: A small pail-shaped mold used to shape rice, custards, mousselines, and other items. Also, a preparation made in such a mold.

Tourné knife: A small knife, similar to a paring knife, with a curved blade used to tourné items.

Utility knife: A smaller, lighter version of the chef's knife; its blade is usually between 5 and 7 inches long.

Vertical chopping machine (VCM): A machine, similar to a blender, that has rotating blades used to grind, whip, emulsify, or blend foods.

Walk-in refrigeration: Large cold storage unit, usually fitted with shelves, to hold large quantities of food.

Whip/whisk: To beat an item, such as cream or egg whites, to incorporate air. Also, a special tool for whipping made of looped wire attached to a handle.

Wok (Chin.): A round-bottomed pan, usually made of rolled steel, that is used for nearly all cooking methods.

Worm: The portion of a meat grinder shaped like the shaft of a screw, used to transfer foods along the feed tube and to the blade of the grinder.

The Raw Ingredients

Objectives

- Describe the availability, quality indicators, common uses, and cooking applications for a wide variety of foods, including:
    - Beef, veal, lamb, pork, and game (pages 105–127)
    - Domestic poultry and game birds (pages 127–130)
    - Fish and shellfish (pages 130–147)
    - Fresh fruits, vegetables, and herbs (pages 147–176)
    - Dairy, cheese, and eggs (pages 176–186)
    - Grains, meals, flours, and dried pastas (pages 187–190 and 192–194)
    - Dried legumes, nuts, and seeds (pages 190–191 and 200–201)
    - Oils, shortenings, vinegars, and condiments (pages 194–197)
    - Extracts, flavorings, wines, cordials, and liqueurs (pages 198–200)
    - Dried herbs and spices (pages 197–198)
    - Sugars, sweeteners, syrups, and chocolate (pages 203–205)
    - Coffees and teas (pages 204, 206)
    - Leaveners and thickeners (pages 206, 208)
    - Frozen and convenience goods (page 208)
- Name the factors taken into account when purchasing ingredients (page 208)
- Describe proper storage techniques for a variety of ingredients (interspersed throughout chapter)

Lecture Outline

TOPIC: Meat and Poultry Identification and Purchasing

MEAT IDENTIFICATION AND PURCHASING
  Meat Basics
    Storage

Inspection and Grading
  Kosher Meats
Market Forms of Meat
Beef
  The Beef Primals
    Chuck
    Rib

Loin
Round
Shank
Flank and Skirt Steak
Brisket
Miscellaneous Cuts of Beef
Oxtail
Heart
Liver
Tongue
Tripe
Veal
Veal Primals and Market Forms
Shoulder (Chuck)
Veal Shank
Rib
Loin
Leg
Breast
Organ Meats/Variety Meats
Pork
Pork Primals and Market Forms
The Shoulder or Butt
The Loin
The Ham (Leg)
Spareribs
Cured Pork and Pork "By-products"
Lamb and Mutton
Venison and Large, Furred Game
- Cuts from less-exercised portions of the animal may be prepared by any technique and are frequently paired with dry-heat methods such as grilling or roasting.
- Well-exercised areas of the animal, such as the leg (or haunch), shank, and shoulder are best when cooked by moist-heat or combination methods. These cuts are also used for preparing pâtés and other charcuterie items.
Rabbit
POULTRY AND GAME BIRDS
Chicken
Cornish Game Hen/Rock Cornish Game Hen
Turkey
Ducks and Geese
Wild Game Birds
Quail

Snipe/Woodcock
Wild Duck
Pheasant

TOPIC: Fish and Shellfish Identification and Purchasing
FISH AND SHELLFISH
Fish Basics
Purchasing
1. Smell the fish.
2. Feel the skin.
3. Look at the fins and tail.
4. Press the flesh.
5. Check the eyes.
6. Check the gills.
7. Check the belly.
8. Check live shellfish for signs of movement.
Storage
1. Check the fish carefully for freshness and quality.
2. Place the fish on a bed of shaved or flaked ice in a perforated container.
3. Cover with additional shaved or flaked ice.
4. Set the perforated container inside a second container.
5. Re-ice fish daily.
Market Forms
Categories
Round fish
Flat fish
Nonbony fish
Shellfish
1. Mollusks
- Univalves (single-shelled), such as abalone and sea urchins
- Bivalves (two shells joined by a hinge), such as clams, mussels, oysters, and scallops
2. Crustaceans (jointed exterior skeletons or shells), such as lobster, shrimp, and crayfish
3. Cephalopods, such as squid and octopus

COMMONLY AVAILABLE FISH
- Round Fish
  - Anchovy
  - Bass
  - Bluefish
  - Catfish
  - Cod
  - Dolphin Fish (Mahi Mahi)
  - Eel
  - Groupers
  - Haddock (see Cod)
  - John Dory
  - Mackerel
  - Monkfish
  - Perch
  - Permit
  - Pike
  - Pompano
  - Puffer
  - Salmon
  - Shad
  - Shark
  - Skate/Ray
  - Snappers
  - Swordfish
  - Tautog
  - Tilapia
  - Tilefish/Golden Bass
  - Trigger Fish
  - Trout
  - Tuna
  - Weakfish
- Flat Fish
  - Dover Sole
  - Flounder
  - Halibut
  - Turbot
- Shellfish
  - Univalves
    - Abalone
    - Conch
    - Snails
  - Bivalves
    - Clams
      - Littlenecks
      - Topnecks
      - Cherrystones
      - Quahogs
      - Pacific littleneck
      - Soft-shell
    - Mussels
    - Oysters
    - Scallops
  - Crustaceans
    - Crab
    - Crayfish
    - Lobster
    - Shrimp
  - Cephalopods
    - Octopus
    - Squid
  - Miscellaneous Items
    - Caviar
    - Frogs' Legs

TOPIC: Fruits and Vegetables Identification and Purchasing

FRUITS
- Apples
- Berries
  - Strawberries
  - Raspberries
  - Blueberries
  - Blackberries
  - Cranberries
- Citrus Fruits
  - Oranges
    - Thin-skinned
    - Thick-skinned
    - Bitter
  - Grapefruits
  - Lemons
  - Limes
  - Oranges
  - Tangerines
- Specialty Fruits
  - Dates
  - Figs
  - Kiwis
  - Mangos

Papayas
Plantains
Pomegranates
Passion fruit
Grapes
Melons
  Cantaloupes
  Watermelons
  Winter melons (Honeydew, Casaba, Crenshaw)
  Muskmelons
Stone Fruits
  Peaches
  Nectarines
  Apricots
  Plums
  Cherries
Pears
Rhubarb

VEGETABLES
Avocados
Cabbage Family
  Broccoli
  Brussels sprouts
  Cauliflower
  Kale
  Kohlrabi
  Collard greens
  Many kinds of cabbage
  (Turnips and rutabagas are also members of this family, but they are more commonly thought of as root vegetables.)
Cooking Greens
Cucumbers, Squashes, and Eggplant
  Squashes
    Summer squashes (Zucchini, Yellow, Crookneck, Pattypan)
    Winter squashes (Acorn, Butternut, Hubbard, Pumpkin, Spaghetti)
Lettuces
Mushrooms
Sidebar Truffles
Onion Family
  Garlic
  Shallots

Dry and green onions
Onions fall into two main categories, reflecting the state in which they are used: cured (dried) and fresh (green).
Peppers, Bell
Peppers, Chili
Sidebar Dried Chili Nomenclature
Pod and Seed Vegetables
  Fresh legumes, such as peas, beans, and bean sprouts
  Corn
  Okra
Potatoes, white
  (Sweet potatoes and yams, themselves unrelated botanically, are also not closely related to the white potato.)
Roots and Tubers:
  Beets
  Carrots
  Celeriac
  Parsnips
  Radishes
  Rutabagas
  Turnips
  Salsify tubers
    Jerusalem artichokes
Shoots and Stalks
Tomatoes
HERBS
Selection
Proper Use
  Storage

TOPIC: Dairy, Cheese, Eggs and Nonperishable Goods Identification
PURCHASING AND STORAGE
Dairy Products
  Milk
  Cream
  Ice Cream
  Butter
  Fermented and Cultured Milk Products
Cheese
  Fresh Cheese
  Soft or Rind-ripened Cheeses

Semi-soft Cheese
Hard Cheeses (Cheddar-type)
Grating Cheeses
Blue-veined Cheese
Eggs
  Basic rules for safe handling:
- All eggs in the shell should be free from cracks, leaking, or obvious holes.
- Eggs should be cooked to a minimum of 165°F (74°C) to kill the salmonella bacteria. Fried eggs or poached eggs with runny yolks should be prepared only at customer request.
- Any foods containing eggs must be kept at safe temperature throughout handling, cooking and storage. Cooling and reheating must be done quickly over direct heat.

Egg whites
Egg yolks
Grading, Sizes, and Market Forms
  Jumbo
  Extra large
  Large
  Medium
  Small
  Pee wee
- Eggs are also sold in several processed forms:
- Bulk, or fluid, whole eggs
- Pasteurized eggs
- Dried, powdered eggs
- Egg substitutes

PURCHASING AND STORAGE OF NONPERISHABLE GOODS
  Grains, Meals, and Flours
  Dried Legumes
  Dried Pasta and Noodles
  Oils and Shortenings
  Vinegars and Condiments
  Dried Herbs and Spices
  Salt and Pepper
  Extracts and Other Flavorings
  Wines, Cordials, and Liqueurs
  Nuts and Seeds
  Dried Fruits and Vegetables

Sugars, Syrups, and Other Sweeteners
Chocolate
Coffee, Tea, and Other Beverages
Leaveners
Thickeners
  Arrowroot
  Cornstarch
  Filé gumbo powder
  Gelatin
Prepared, Canned, and Frozen Foods
SUMMARY

Discussion Topics

TOPIC: Selecting ingredients based on clientele/cost
- Fresh vs. frozen
- Fresh vs. dried
- Made in-house vs. convenience foods
- Organic vs. non-organic
- Items available (produce) from other countries (availability vs. quality)
- Seasonal vs. year round availability

Resource: Video

Food Purchasing I and II: General Principles, *National Education Media*

TOPIC: Moral issues regarding veal, lamb, game, rabbit

TOPIC: Fish farming: aquaculture
- Pros and cons
- Depleting the resources
- Quality
- Trash/junk fish gaining in popularity

TOPIC: Organic farming
- Difficulty in producing enough for stores and restaurants
- Honesty in labeling
- Chef's Collaborative 2000

Resource: Video

(Alice Waters at Chez Panisse) A Moveable Feast (Smithsonian World), *WETA & The Smithsonian Institute*

TOPIC: Genetic engineering

TOPIC: Irradiation

TOPIC: New products/produce
• Read, read, read
• Newly created items
• Ethnic items which are becoming popular

Resource: Magazines

Chef, "Product Gallery"
Saveur, "The Pantry" and "Source"
Eating Well, "Marketplace"
Food and Wine, "Selects"

Resource: Videos

Foodservice: Handling and Evaluation of Seafood. *National Fisheries Institute*, (202) 296-3428.
Chilies: Identification and Preparation. *Culinary Institute of America*, 1996.

Resource: Book

The Meat Buyer's Guide. National Association of Meat Purveyors. Reston, Virginia, 1992.
SPECS: The Comprehensive Foodservice Purchasing and Specifications Manual. Lewis Reed. Van Nostrand Reinhold. New York, 1993.
Quality Food Purchasing. Kotschevar and Levinson. Macmillan. New York, 1988.

Assignments

1 The fish that were delivered yesterday now smell rotten, despite the fact that they were immediately iced down. What can be done to prevent this in the future?
   • Check the fish when they are received
     They should smell fresh.
     The skin should feel slick and moist.
     Fins and tail should be moist and flexible.
     The flesh should be firm and elastic.
     Eyes should be clear and full.
   • If the fish does not meet this criteria, it should not be accepted.
   • See also pages 131–133.

2 The guest returned the poached bluefish, saying that it had an unpleasant flavor and texture. The fish was very fresh and of high quality when the chef checked it immediately before cooking.
   • Customer not familiar with bluefish
   • Cooking technique may have tended to highlight strong flavor
   • See also pages 130–131, 135–136, 138.

3 The salsa made with fresh tomatoes is usually so popular that is is difficult to keep the customers supplied fast enough. Ever since summer ended, though, demand for salsa has fallen off. Why? And how could you increase the demand?
   • Hot house tomatoes do not have as much flavor as fresh summer tomatoes. Try improving the flavor of the salsa by:
     Roasting or smoking the fresh tomatoes
     Adding some canned plum tomatoes
     Adding some tomato juice
   • See also pages 157–158, 172–173.

4 A bunch of bananas was left near a basket of ripe peaches. The next day the peaches were rotten. Why?
   • Bananas give off the gas ethylene which causes fruit to ripen.
   • See also page 152.

5 The milk and cream kept at the waiter's station for coffee and tea are frequently left out during the entire service period. Even though the

date stamps say the milk should be wholesome and safe to serve, it curdles as soon as it is poured into a hot beverage.

- Obviously, the milk and cream has gone bad. It should be kept under refrigeration or on ice, if that is more convenient, during service time.
- Even if it is early in service and the containers were just filled, they must be kept iced. Someone may have "married" the milk or cream from several containers. This contaminates fresh milk or cream.
- See also pages 176–177.

6 The soup made from black beans was gritty, with a moldy flavor. What might have caused this?
- The beans were old
- The beans were not picked through
- The beans were not washed before cooking
- See also pages 188–190.

7 Even though the rump roast of venison has a good flavor, it is tough and hard to chew. It seems dry, also.
- It may have been overcooked.
- It would be more tender and moist if it had been braised.

8 The new chef decides to purchase fresh avocados and discontinue using the frozen guacamole that the coffee shop was previously using on the taco salad. Because of the expense, he must raise the cost of the salad and sales drop. He ends up throwing away half a case of rotten avocados. Was his decision a sound one?
- For his purposes—a dollop of guacamole on the top of a taco salad—the chef might have been better off using the frozen guacamole. Perhaps his customers did not value the fresh avocados.
- The chef could have introduced a few specials such as a guacamole salad appetizer, turkey and avocado sandwich, and Cobb salad to use the avocados before they went bad.
- See also pages 158–159.

9 Many people are simply not confident about purchasing meats and fish and cooking them at home. They fear that they will not get the right amount, or that the meat or fish will be tough and dry after they cook it. Consequently, they would almost rather go to a restaurant for a cut of meat or fish that they aren't sure about preparing. What meats and fish are especially likely to be popular on a menu, though not necessarily at home? Why?
- Variety meats, all—difficult, lack of experience
- Prime rib—size, expensive
- Steamship round—size, long cooking time, inadequate equipment
- Game and rabbit—lack of experience
- Rack of lamb—difficult, expensive, lack of experience
- Lamb shank—difficult, lack of experience
- Veal shank—Osso buco—difficult, lack of experience, long cooking time
- Whole fish—difficult, lack of experience, cutting, preparation
- Shellfish—clams, mussels, oysters—difficult, time consuming, lack of experience, involves killing the fish
- Lobster—difficult, expensive, lack of experience, involves killing the lobster
- Soft-shelled crab—difficult, expensive, time-consuming, lack of experience, sometimes involves killing the crab
- Crab—difficult, perceived as expensive, time-consuming, lack of experience, involves killing the crab
- Snails—difficult, time-consuming, lack of experience
- Sushi, sashimi—difficult, time-consuming, lack of experience, safety concern
- See also pages 108–112, 116, 123–127, 135–146.

10 Several factors have contributed to make fish and shellfish increasingly popular menu items. Discuss the ways in which new thinking about lifestyle, fitness, diet, and health have contributed to a growing demand for fish and shellfish.
- Omega-3 fatty acids and link to cardiovascular health

- Popularity in "healthy" cuisines (Pacific Rim, Mediterranean)
- Naturally lower in total fat, especially saturated fats and cholesterol
- See also pages 64–65, 69–72, 130.

11 As fish continues to grow in popularity, there has been increasing difficulty in meeting the demand for many of the more commonly known and "popular" fish. What is being done to meet the growing demand from consumers? How can the chef sell fish profitably, while taking full advantage of the range of fish and shellfish available in the market?

- Fish farming (aquaculture) is becoming big business; more fish are available, although some chefs believe farmed fish is less flavorful
- Chefs can begin to use "trash fish," such as roughy and tilapia
- Use purveyor as information resource regarding qualities and properties of fish (texture, flavor, lean vs. oil)

12 Several key contemporary figures have raised the status of vegetables and fruits from an afterthought to the main focus of a plate. How has the work of people like Alice Waters and Larry Forgione influenced not only the ways in which fruits and vegetables are used, but also the ways in which they are being grown throughout the country?

- There is more demand for fresh, seasonal produce rather than year-round availability of tasteless produce.
- Many restaurants are hiring farmers to grow directly for them (boutique farming).
- Increase in popularity of farmer's markets.
- See also page 16.

13 Dairy products, especially cheeses and butter, have come under nutritional fire in recent years. How might this affect the way you purchase and use these items in the kitchen?

- Cheeses and butter can be used sparingly in the kitchen.
- Butter can be replaced (sometimes) by olive oil.
- Consider using sharp or pungent cheeses for flavor when possible: one ounce of gorgon-

zola or parmesan will give more flavor than four ounces of colby.
- See also pages 177–184.

Answer Key to Self-Study Questions

1 Beef: Prime, Choice, Select
Veal: Prime, Choice, Good
Lamb: Prime, Choice, Good
Pork: U.S. Nos. 1, 2, 3, 4, Utility.

2 • Marbling—the more marbling, the more tender the meat
- Exercise of the muscle—the more exercised, the tougher the meat
- Cooking method—long, slow cooking applications tenderize tougher meats

3 • Shape of the carcass
- Ratio of meat to bone
- Freedom from pinfeathers, hair, and down
- Number (if any) of tears, cuts, or broken bones.

4 • The characteristics of game birds are not reproductively controlled.
- The characteristics of domesticated poultry are reproductively controlled.
- Game birds are generally at their best from October through January, though they may be available year-round.
- The quality of domesticated poultry remains fairly constant throughout the year.

5 • Rock Cornish game hen, broiler, fryer, roaster, and young hen or tom turkey are suitable for all cooking techniques.
- Yearling turkey, roaster duckling, young goose/gosling, and broiler/fryer duckling are usually roasted.
- Capon may be roasted or poêléed.
- Stewing hens require slow, moist cooking.
- Guinea hen or fowl is suitable for most techniques.
- Squab may be sautéed, roasted, or grilled.

6 (1) Smell for a clean aroma
(2) Feel the skin for slickness, moistness, and flexibility
(3) Check the fins and tail for moistness and fullness

(4) Press the flesh for firmness and elasticity

(5) Check the eyes; they should be clear and full

(6) Check the gills for good red-to-maroon color

(7) Check the belly for unbroken flesh with no signs of belly burn

(8) Check live shellfish for signs of movement

7 *Whole fish:*

(1) Rinse the fish

(2) Place on a bed of shaved or flaked ice in a perforated container (for round fish, fill the belly cavity with ice and place belly-down; a flat fish should be placed on its side)

(3) Cover with additional shaved or flaked ice, layer if necessary

(4) Set the perforated container inside a second container to drain away the melted ice

(5) Re-ice the fish daily

Clams, mussels, and oysters:
- Stored in the bag in which they were delivered, in the refrigerator, un-iced and weighted down

Scallops out of the shell and fish fillets:
- Stored in metal containers set over ice, but not touching the ice

Crabs, lobsters and other live shellfish:
- Packed in seaweed and stored in their shipping containers under refrigeration

Frozen fish and shrimp:
- Kept frozen until they are ready to be thawed and cooked.

8 Shaved or flaked ice makes a tighter seal around the entire fish and slows the loss of quality without bruising the flesh.

9
- Garlic
- Shallots
- Scallions (green onions)
- Ramps
- Leeks
- Cippolini onions
- Boiling onions
- Pearl onions
- Red onions
- Spanish onions
- Sweet onions (Walla Walla, Vidalia, Maui)
- Yellow onions
- White onions

10
- Beluga—large grain and light in color
- Ship—medium grain and light in color
- Sevruga—small grain and dark colored
- Osetra—small grained and dark

11 Will Continue to Ripen:

Bananas, melons, pears, plums, peaches, nectarines

Won't Continue to Ripen

Pineapples, apples, berries, cherries, grapes, lemons

12
- Clingstone—flesh clings to the pit.
- Freestone—flesh separates easily from the pit.

13
- Tubers are enlarged, bulbous sections of a plant's root structure, and are capable of generating new plants.
- Roots are not capable of generating new plants.

14
- Wrap them loosely in damp paper or cloth and place in plastic bags under refrigeration, or trim stems and place in a jar of water, wrapped with damp paper towels under refrigeration
- Use with discretion, so as to not overwhelm the flavors of a dish
- Cutting should be done as close to serving time as possible
- Addition to cooked preparations should be timed so that they cook long enough to meld with other ingredients, but not so far in advance that the flavors cook out

15
- Fresh cheese—moist, soft, mild flavor
- Soft or rind-ripened cheese—surface mold and an edible, soft velvety skin; ripens from the outside to the center, runny with full flavor when perfectly ripe
- Semi-soft cheese—more solid than soft, but does not grate easily; coated with inedible wax rind, aged for specific periods of time
- Hard or cheddar-type cheese—drier texture and firm consistency; slices and grates easily

- Grating cheese—crumbly texture, perfect for shaving or grating
- Blue-veined cheese—varied consistencies, ranging from smooth and creamy to dry and crumbly, injected with mold.

16 Inoculating milk or cream with a bacterial strain that causes fermentation to begin; fermentation process thickens the milk and gives it a pleasantly sour flavor.

17
- Ability to foam
- Formation of emulsions
- Addition of richness
- Add color, structure, and flavor

18 Oils they contain may become rancid at room temperature.

19 Please see Table 5–38 on pages 187–188 for a complete listing of grains, their purchase forms, and major uses or dishes.

20
- Clarified butter: 95°F (36°C), 300°F (150°C)
- Sunflower oil: 2°F (−17°C), 440°F (225°C)
- Lard: 92°F (33°C), 375°F (190°C)
- Corn oil: 12°F (−11°C), 450°F (230°C)

Keywords

Aged beef: Beef allowed to hang in a climate-controlled area for a period of time in order to allow enzymes to act on meat fibers, changing texture, flavor, and color of meat.

Ante-mortem: An inspection of meats and poultry after they have been slaughtered to assure that the food is wholesome, safe, and fit for human consumption.

Aquaculture: The cultivation or farm-raising of fish or shellfish.

Bivalve: A mollusk with two hinged shells. Examples are clams and oysters.

Boxed meat: Meat which has been slaughtered, butchered, packaged, and boxed before being shipped to purveyors, retailers, and restaurants.

Cephalopod: Marine creatures whose tentacles and arms are attached directly to their heads; includes squid and octopus.

Chocolate liquor: The paste resulting from the crushing of the cocoa bean.

Cocoa powder: The pods of the cacao tree, processed to remove the cocoa butter and ground into powder. Used as a flavoring.

Condiment: An aromatic mixture, such as pickles, chutney, and some sauces and relishes, that accompanies food (usually kept on the table throughout service).

Cryovac®: A packaging system in which foods are packed in airtight plastic after processing to minimize contamination from the point of processing until the food reaches its final destination.

Culture: A bacterial strain that induces foods to undergo a change; often used to produce such dairy items as sour cream, cheese, and buttermilk.

Curds: Milk solids that have formed into a mass; a stage in cheese production.

Cutability: A term used to indicate the overall ratio of usable meat to bones and trim.

Date stamp: A labeling system used to indicate the last date on which an item is still fresh, wholesome, and suitable for sale in an unopened container. This assumes that the product was held and stored properly throughout processing, shipping, and all subsequent handling.

Emulsion: (1) A flavoring made by steeping aromatic substances in an oil.
(2) The suspension of an oil in water (or the reverse).

Ethylene gas: A gas emitted by various fruits and vegetables; ethylene gas speeds ripening, maturing, and, eventually, rotting.

Extracts: A flavoring made by steeping aromatic substances in alcohol.

Fermentation: The breakdown of carbohydrates into carbon dioxide gas and alcohol, usually through the action of yeast on sugar.

Flat fish: A fish skeletal type characterized by its flat body and both eyes on one side of its head (for example, sole, plaice, and halibut).

Foie gras (Fr.): The fattened liver of a duck or goose.

Free-range: Livestock that is raised unconfined.

Government inspection: Inspection of foodstuffs to be sure that they meet all appropriate standards for purity, wholesomeness, and safety.

Hanging meat: Meat primals or subprimals that are delivered unboxed; typically allowed to hang from hooks with air circulating around them.

Homogenization; homogenized: A process used to prevent the milkfat from separating out of milk products. The liquid is forced through an ultrafine mesh at high pressure, which breaks up fat globules, dispersing them evenly throughout the liquid.

Kosher meat: Butchered and prepared in accordance with Jewish dietary laws.

Legume: The seeds of certain plants, including beans and peas, which are eaten for their earthy flavors and high nutritional value. Also, the French word for vegetable.

Marbling: The intramuscular fat found in meat that makes the meat tender and juicy.

Milkfat/butterfat: The fat content of fluid milk; typically expressed as a percentage.

Milled grains: Grains that have been processed by grinding or milling.

Mollusk: Any of a number of invertebrate animals with soft, unsegmented bodies usually enclosed in a hard shell; included are clams, oysters, and snails.

Natural cheese: A cheese that is considered "living." The texture and flavor will continue to change as the cheese ages.

Offal: Variety meats, including organs (brains, heart, kidneys, liver or lungs, sweetbreads, tripe, tongue), head meat, tail, and feet.

Oil: A type of cooking fat that is liquid (pourable) at room temperature; produced by extracting fats from vegetables, seeds, nuts or beans.

Pasteurization: A process in which milk products are heated to kill microorganisms that could contaminate the milk.

Post-mortem: Inspection of animals prior to slaughter to ensure that they are safe, wholesome, and fit for human consumption.

Primal cuts: The portions produced by the initial cutting of an animal carcass. Cuts are determined standards that may vary from country to country and animal type to type. Primal cuts are further broken down into smaller, more manageable cuts.

Quality grading: The assignment of grades to carcasses based on various standards, including ratio of meat to bone, marbling, etc. A practice paid for by meat packers and processors.

Round fish: A classification of fish based on skeletal type, characterized by a rounded body and eyes on opposite sides of its head.

Shortening: A cooking fat that is solid at room temperature; made by adding hydrogen molecules to an oil in a process called hydrogenization.

Subprimals/retail cuts: Term used to describe cuts of meat produced from primal cuts.

Ultrapasteurization: Procedure for pasteurizing dairy products at very high temperatures for short periods of time.

Univalve: A single-shelled mollusk, such as abalone and sea urchin.

USDA: United State Department of Agriculture; a large branch of the federal government charged with (among other things) overseeing the production, distribution, labeling, inspection, and sales of food items to the public.

Vinegar: A highly fermented juice made from fruits, wine, or grains.

Whey: The liquid left after curds have formed in milk.

White chocolate: Cocoa butter flavored with sugar and milk solids. It does not contain any cocoa solids, so it does not have the characteristic brown color of regular chocolate.

Whole grains: Unmilled or unprocessed grains.

Yield grade: An indication of the overall ratio of usable meat to bone on an individual carcass.

CHAPTER 6

Mise en Place

Objectives

- Understand a variety of basic knife cuts, including a few decorative cuts (pages 217–223)
- Peel and/or cut a variety of specific vegetables (pages 223–235)
- Work properly with a variety of dried fruits, vegetables, and beans (pages 235–236 and 200–202)
- Prepare and use a number of thickeners (pages 238–240)
- Prepare and use a number of aromatic and flavoring combinations (pages 241–245)
- Explain the categories of stocks, broths, and court bouillons and describe the correct methods of preparing, storing, and using them (pages 245–253)
- Execute a number of basic cooking techniques, including:
    Rendering and clarifying fats (pages 253–254)
    Preparing foams and folding them into a base (pages 254–257)
    Preparing parchment cones and liners (pages 259-260)
    Separating eggs (page 254)
    Tempering ingredients (pages 257–258)
    Straining sauces (pages 258–259)
- Fabricate a variety of cuts of beef, veal, lamb, pork, and game into serving preparations, including:
    Tying a roast (pages 264–265)
    Butterflying (page 266)
    Frenching (pages 262, 266)
    Pounding (page 261)
    Boning (pages 266 and 268–269)
    Cleaning and trimming (page 261)
- Fabricate poultry, into the following preparations:
    Trussing (pages 272–273)
    Cutting whole birds into portions (pages 273–277)
    Preparing suprêmes (pages 275–277)
- Fabricate a variety of fish and shellfish into serving preparations, including:
    Scaling, trimming, and gutting (pages 278–279)
    Pan-dressing (pages 279–280)

Shucking mollusks (page 288)
Filleting (pages 280–284)
Peeling and deveining (page 284)

Lecture Outline

TOPIC: Knife Skills and Basic Mise en Place
Knife Skills
  Holding the Knife
    The three basic grips used with a chef's knife are as follows:
    1. Grip the handle with all four fingers and hold the thumb gently but firmly on top of the blade.
    2. Grip the handle with four fingers and hold the thumb firmly against the side of the blade.
    3. Grip the handle with three fingers, resting the index finger flat against the blade on one side, and holding the thumb on the opposite side to give additional stability and control for finer cuts.
  The Guiding Hand
  Basic Knife Cuts
    • Coarse chopping and mincing
    • Mincing
    • Shredding (chiffonade)
    • Julienne and bâtonnet
    • Dicing
    • Paysanne or fermière
    • Lozenge
    • Rondelle
    • Oblique, or roll cut
  Peeling Vegetables and Fruits
  Coarse Chopping
    1. Trim the root and stem ends and peel if necessary.
    2. Slice or chop at nearly regular intervals until the cuts are relatively uniform.
  Mincing
    1. Gather herbs or roughly chopped garlic or shallots in a pile on a cutting board and position the knife above the pile.
    2. Keeping the tip of the blade against the cutting board, raise and lower the knife's heel firmly and rapidly, repeatedly chopping through the herbs or vegetables.
    3. Continue chopping until desired fineness is attained.
  Chiffonade/Shredding
    1. When cutting tight heads of greens, such as Belgian endive or head cabbage, core the head and cut it in half, if it is large, to make cutting easier. For greens with large, loose leaves, roll individual leaves into tight cylinders before cutting. For smaller leaves, stack several leaves on top of one another.
    2. Use a chef's knife to make very fine, parallel cuts to produce fine shreds. A box grater or mandolin can also be used to cut items such as cabbages or head lettuce.
  Julienne and Bâtonnet
    1. Trim the vegetable so that the sides are straight, which will make it easier to produce even cuts. (The trimmings can be used, as appropriate, for stocks, soups, purées, or any preparation where the shape is not important.)
    2. Slice the vegetable lengthwise, using parallel cuts of the proper thickness.
    3. Stack the slices, aligning the edges, and make parallel cuts of the same thickness through the stack. To make bâtonnet, the cuts should be thick. To make a fine julienne, the cuts should be very thin.
  Dice
    1. Trim and cut the vegetable as for julienne or bâtonnet.
    2. Gather the julienne or bâtonnets and cut through them crosswise at evenly spaced intervals.

Paysanne/Fermière
1. Trim and cut the vegetable as for bâtonnet.
2. Make even, thin, crosswise cuts in the bâtonnets, at roughly ¼-inch intervals.

Lozenge/Diamond
1. Trim and slice the vegetable thinly.
2. Cut the slices into strips of the desired width.
3. Make an initial bias cut to begin the process. This will leave some trim that should be reserved for use in preparations that do not require a neat, decorative cut.
4. Continue to make bias cuts, parallel to the first one.

Rondelles/Rounds
1. Trim and peel the vegetable if necessary.
2. Make parallel slicing cuts through the vegetable at even intervals.

Diagonal/Bias Cut
1. Place the peeled or trimmed vegetable on the work surface.
2. Make a series of even parallel cuts on the bias.

Oblique or Roll Cut
1. Place the peeled vegetable on a cutting board. Make a diagonal cut to remove the stem end.
2. Hold the knife in the same position and roll the vegetable 180 degrees (a half-turn). Slice through it on the same diagonal, forming a piece with two angled edges.
3. Repeat until the entire vegetable has been cut.

Turned (Tournéed) Vegetables
1. Peel the vegetable, if desired.
2. Cut into pieces of manageable size. Cut large round or oval vegetables, such as beets and potatoes, into quarters, sixths, or eighths (depending on their size), to form pieces slightly larger than 2 inches. Cut cylindrical vegetables, such as carrots, into 2-inch pieces.
3. Using a paring or tourné knife, carve the pieces into barrel or football shapes. The faces should be smooth, evenly spaced, and tapered so that both ends are narrower than the center.

Sidebar Special and Decorative Cuts Using Special Cutting Tools and Techniques
Fluting
Fanning

ADVANCE PREPARATION TECHNIQUES FOR CERTAIN VEGETABLES
Onions
Peeling and Dicing an Onion
1. Use a paring knife to remove the stem end. Peel off the skin and the underlying layer, if it contains brown spots. Trim the root end but leave it intact.
2. Halve the onion lengthwise through the root. Lay it cut-side down and make a series of evenly spaced, parallel, lengthwise cuts with the tip of a chef's knife, again leaving the root end intact. The closer the cuts, the finer the dice will be.
3. Make two or three horizontal cuts parallel to the work surface, from the onion's stem end toward the root end, but do not cut all the way through.
4. Make even, crosswise cuts with a chef's knife, all the way through, from stem to root end.

Garlic and Shallots
Peeling and Mashing Garlic and Shallots
1. To loosen the skin, crush the garlic clove or shallot bulb between the knife blade's flat side and the cutting board, using the heel of the hand. Peel off the skin and remove the root end and any brown spots.
2. Mince the clove or bulb fairly fine, or coarsely chop, as for herbs.
3. Hold the knife at an angle and use the cutting edge to mash the garlic or shallot against the cutting board. Repeat this step until the item is mashed to a paste.
4. To hold, place in a jar, cover with a layer of oil, and refrigerate.

Roasting Garlic and Shallots

1. Place the unpeeled head of garlic or shallot bulbs in a small pan or sizzler platter.
2. Roast at a moderate temperature until the garlic or shallots are quite soft.

Leeks

Tomatoes

Preparing Tomato Concassé

1. Cut an "X" into the bottom of the tomato.
2. Bring a pot of water to a rolling boil. Drop the tomatoes into the water. After 10 to 30 seconds, remove them with a slotted spoon, skimmer, or spider. Immediately plunge them into very cold or ice water. Pull away the skin.
3. Halve each tomato crosswise at its widest point and gently squeeze out the seeds.
4. Coarsely chop or cut the flesh into dice or julienne, as desired.

Roasting Tomatoes

1. Core the tomato and cut it into halves or slices.
2. Coat lightly with oil, and add seasonings and aromatics as desired. Salt, pepper, fresh or dried herbs, plain or infused oils, chopped garlic, or shallots are all good choices.
3. Roast the tomatoes until they are browned and have a rich "roasted" aroma.

Sweet Peppers and Chilies

Seeding and Cutting Peppers

Roasting and Peeling Peppers

Peeling with a swivel peeler

1. Section the pepper with a knife, cutting along the folds to expose the unpeeled skin.
2. Remove the core, seeds, and ribs, and peel with a swivel peeler.

Charred peppers

1. Hold the pepper over the flame of a gas burner with tongs or a kitchen fork or place the pepper on a grill.

Turn the pepper and roast it until the surface is evenly charred.
2. Place in a plastic or paper bag or under an inverted bowl to steam the skin loose.
3. When the pepper is cool enough to handle, remove the charred skin, using a paring knife if necessary.

Oven- or broiler-roasted peppers

1. Halve the peppers and remove stems and seeds. Place cut-side down on an oiled sheet pan.
2. Place in a very hot oven or under a broiler. Roast or broil until evenly charred.
3. Remove from the oven or broiler and cover immediately, using an inverted sheet pan. This will steam the peppers, making the skin easier to remove.
4. Peel, using a paring knife if necessary.

Deep-fried peppers

1. Using tongs or the double-basket method, submerge the peppers in oil that has been heated to 325°F (165°C).
2. Deep-fry the peppers for about a minute, until they are blistered all over. The peppers usually will not brown dramatically.
3. Remove from the deep fat, drain, and let cool.
4. Peel away the skin, using a paring knife if necessary.

Mushrooms

Leafy Greens

1. Fill a sink with cool water. Separate or loosen heading greens and dip them into the water. Plunge them in and out of the water to loosen the sand.
2. Lift them out of the water, and drain the sink. Repeat the process until there are no signs of grit remaining in the water.
3. Once rinsed, allow the greens to drain briefly and, if necessary, spin them dry using a salad spinner.

Fresh Herbs
Citrus Fruits
  Zesting Citrus Fruit
    1. Use a paring knife, swivel-bladed peeler, or zester to remove only the peel's colored portion.
    2. If julienne or grated zest is called for, use a chef's knife to cut or mince the zest. Grated zest can also be prepared using the fine holes of a box grater.
Chestnuts
Eggplant
  Salting Eggplant
    1. Slice the ends from the eggplant and discard, or slice it in half from one end to the other. Slice or score the eggplant as required by recipe or desired result.
    2. Scatter salt liberally over the eggplant, tossing slices to coat them evenly.
    3. Place the eggplant in a colander or perforated hotel pan, and (optional) weight the eggplant to help expel the juices.
    4. Rinse the eggplant well to remove the salt, dry thoroughly, and then proceed with cooking.
  Roasting Eggplant
    1. Slice the eggplant in half lengthwise.
    2. Score it in a diamond pattern, cutting through most of the flesh, but leaving the skin intact.
    3. If desired, rub the cut surface with some olive oil.
    4. Roast the eggplant cut-side down until softened but not browned.
    5. Turn the eggplant cut-side up, and continue to roast until the flesh is very soft. It is now ready to purée. If desired, the flesh can be strained after puréeing.
Corn
  Removing Kernals
    Hold ear upright and cut down the rows.
  "Milking" Corn
    1. Score the rows of kernels with a knife.
    2. Use the back of a knife, a spoon, or a butter curler to scrape out the flesh.

Potatoes
Artichokes
    1. Use a sharp knife to cut away the very top and the stem of the artichoke. Rub the cut surface with lemon to prevent discoloration.
    2. Use kitchen shears to snip off the barbs that remain on the leaves. The choke can be scooped out now if desired.
    3. (Optional) Use twine to hold the artichoke's shape. Or, lemon slices or juice can be added to the cooking water.
Snow and Sugar Snap Peas
Asparagus
Apples

TOPIC: Other Basic Preparations
  Working with Dried Fruits and Vegetables
    1. Check the dried ingredient first, to remove any obvious debris or seriously blemished, moldy specimens.
    2. Place it in a bowl or other container and add enough boiling or very hot liquid to cover.
    3. Let the dried ingredient steep in the hot water for several minutes, until softened and plumped.
    4. Pour off the liquid, reserving it if desired for use in another preparation. If necessary, the liquid can be strained through a coffee filter or cheesecloth to remove any debris.
  Soaking Beans
    The Long-Soak Method:
      1. Place the rinsed and sorted beans in a container and add enough cool water to cover them by a few inches.
      2. Let the beans soak for the suggested period (time will vary depending upon the bean from 4 to 24 hours).
      3. Drain the beans, and continue to cook as directed.
    Quick-Soak Method:
      1. Place the rinsed and sorted beans in a pot, and add enough water to cover by a few inches. Bring the water to a simmer.

2. Remove the pot from direct heat and cover. Let the beans steep for an hour.

3. Drain, and continue cooking as directed by recipe.

Making Bread Crumbs

Making Croutons

Toasting Nuts and Seeds

Additional Basic Mise en Place and Appareil

Thickeners

 Slurries

1. Blend the starch thoroughly with one to two times its volume of cold liquid.

2. Bring the hot liquid to a simmer or a low boil.

3. Gradually add the slurry, stirring or whisking constantly to prevent lumping and scorching.

4. Bring the liquid back to a boil and cook just until the sauce reaches the desired thickness and clarity.

 Beurre Manié

1. Allow the butter to soften until it is pliable but not melted—it should still be cool and "plastic."

2. Add an equal weight of flour and work to a smooth paste.

3. If the beurre manié will not be used right away, store it, tightly wrapped, in the refrigerator.

Roux

• White roux: barely colored, or chalky.

• Pale or blond roux: a golden straw color, with a slightly nutty aroma.

• Brown roux: deep brown, with a strong nutty aroma.

• Dark brown or "black" roux; very dark brown to black with a strong charred, almost burned aroma.

 Preparing a Roux

1. Melt the butter or other fat in a pan over moderate to low heat.

2. Add the flour and stir until smooth.

3. If necessary, add a small amount of flour to achieve the proper consistency.

4. Cook, stirring constantly, to the desired color. Roux should be glossy in appearance.

5. If the roux will not be used right away, cool and store it, tightly wrapped, in the refrigerator.

 Combining Roux with Liquid

1. Be sure that the roux and liquid temperatures are different—hot liquid and cold roux or cold liquid and hot roux—to help prevent lumping. Add one to the other gradually and whip constantly to work out lumps.

2. Gradually return the soup or sauce to a boil, whisking occasionally.

3. Reduce the heat and simmer, stirring occasionally, at least 20 minutes, to cook out the taste of the flour.

 Liaison

 Gelatin

1. Soak the gelatin in cool liquid before using. This process, called "blooming," allows the gelatin to soften and to begin absorption of the liquid.

2. Melt the dissolved gelatin crystals.

3. Combine the dissolved gelatin with the liquid. Stir well to disperse throughout the mixture. Chill until the mixture is set.

Pâte à Choux (See Chapter 12)

Basic Aromatic and Flavoring Combinations

Sidebar Salt And Pepper Mix

 Spice Blends

 Mirepoix

  White Mirepoix

  Matignon

 Bouquet Garni

 Sachet d' Epices

 Oignon Piqué and Oignon Brulé

 Marinades

• Oil and acid marinades

• Oil and aromatic marinades

• Acid and aromatic marinades

• Dry marinades and rubs

Liquid Marinades

    1. Prepare the ingredient(s) to be marinated and place it (them) in a hotel pan large enough to hold the ingredient(s) comfortably.

    2. Add the marinade and turn the ingredient(s) to coat evenly.

    3. Marinate for the length of time indicated by the recipe, type of main product, or desired result.

Dry Marinades and Rubs

Duxelles

Pesto and Other Herb Pastes

Persillade

TOPIC: Stocks, Broths, Court Bouillons, and Basic Cooking Techniques

Basic Culinary Preparations, per Escoffier

- Stocks and broths used for soups;
- Brown and white stocks used for sauces and thickened gravies;
- Fumets and essences used to flavor the so-called "small sauces."

Categories and Types of Stocks

    White Stock

    Brown Stock

    Remouillage

    Broth (or Bouillon)

    Fumet (or Essence)

    Court Bouillon

Sidebar *Remouillage*

Sidebar *Estouffade*

    Ratios for Stocks

        Beef, Veal, Poultry, Game, or Special Stocks (e.g., Pork or Turkey)

        Fish Stock or Fumet

    Preparing Stocks

        Mise en Place

        1. Assemble all ingredients required for stocks.

- Cool water
- The major flavoring components
- Aromatics and other flavoring ingredients

        2. Assemble all equipment necessary for preparing stocks.

Advance Preparation for Bones

    Blanching Bones

    1. Place the bones in a large pot and add enough cool water to cover them by several inches.

    2. Bring the water to a full boil, and skim any scum that rises to the surface.

    3. Drain away or pour off the cooking liquid, and rinse the bones to remove any scum that may have been trapped by the bones themselves.

    4. The bones are now properly blanched and ready to use in preparing a white stock.

    Browning Bones and Mirepoix

    1. Rinse the bones if necessary and dry them well to remove any excess moisture.

    2. Heat a roasting pan in a hot oven, and add the bones in an even layer.

    3. Roast the bones until they are a rich brown color.

    4. Add the mirepoix and the tomato product to the pan.

    5. Remove the bones from the roasting pan to the stockpot, and deglaze the roasting pan to retain as much of the flavor released as drippings in the final stock as possible.

Method for Preparing Stocks and Broths

    1. Combine the bones with cold water, and bring the water slowly to a boil.

    2. Add the flavoring ingredients at the correct point.

    3. Simmer the stock long enough to fully develop flavor, body, clarity, color, and aroma.

- Brown and white veal stock normally requires 6 to 8 hours of simmering time.
- White beef stock may be simmered for 8 to 10 hours.
- White and brown poultry stocks (including chicken, duck, turkey, pheasant, and so forth) should be allowed

a minimum of 3 hours simmering time.

- Fish stock, fumets, and essences are properly cooked within 30 minutes to an hour.

4. Properly strain, cool, and store the stock, if it is not intended for immediate use.

Basic Cooking Techniques
Methods for Rendering and Clarifying Fats
Rendering Fats

1. Cube the fat, if necessary.
2. Place the fat in a sauteuse. Add about ½ inch of water to the uncooked fats if there are no drippings present.
3. Cook over low heat until the water evaporates and the fat is released. (This is the actual clarifying process.)
4. Remove the cracklings, if any, with a slotted spoon.
5. Use the clarified fat or store it under refrigeration. A caramelized fond from a roast's drippings should remain that is incorporated into pan gravies.

Clarifying Butter

1. Melt the butter in a heavy saucepan over moderate heat.
2. Continue to cook over low heat until the butterfat becomes very clear and the milk solids drop to the bottom of the pot.
3. Skim the surface foam as the butter clarifies.
4. Pour or ladle off the butterfat into another container, being careful to leave all of the liquid in the pan bottom. Discard the liquid.

Sidebar *Alternate Method for Clarifying Butter*
Method for Separating Eggs

1. Crack open the egg over a small bowl.
2. Transfer the egg back and forth between the halves of the shell, letting the white drop into the small bowl.
3. Place the yolk in its container.
4. Inspect the egg white. If the white is clean, transfer it to the whites container. If there

are traces of yolk, reserve it separately for use in omelets, quiches, and other preparations.

Methods for Whipping Ingredients to Make a Foam
Egg Whites

1. Begin whipping the egg whites by hand or machine at moderate speed. Tilt the bowl to make whipping by hand easier, resting the bowl on a folded towel to prevent slipping.
2. When the whites are quite foamy, increase the speed.
3. Whip to the appropriate stage. Ingredients like cream of tartar or sugar can be added to the foam as it develops. It is generally not recommended that they be added before at least the soft peak stage is reached.
   - Soft peak
   - Medium peak
   - Stiff peak

Making Meringues

Soft meringue: Made by whipping egg whites with granulated, superfine, or "bar" sugar.

Swiss (or hard) meringue: Made by incorporating a higher proportion of sugar than is required for a soft meringue.

Italian meringue: Prepared by gradually beating a sugar syrup (cooked to 238°F/114°C) into whites already at soft peak stage.

Whipping Cream
Methods for Folding Foams into a Base Appareil

1. Have the base appareil in a large bowl to accommodate the folding motion. Stir or beat this mixture to soften it, especially if it has been refrigerated for any length of time.
2. Add about one-third of the beaten egg whites or cream and fold in, using a circular motion, going from the side to the bottom of the bowl and back up to the surface.

3. Add the remaining whipped item in one or two additional stages, folding just until blended.

Methods for Tempering

1. Place the liaison in a container, and blend until smooth.
2. Gradually add the hot liquid, a ladleful at a time, whipping constantly.
3. When enough hot liquid has been added to raise the temperature of the liaison, add it back to the pot.
4. Return the pot to direct heat and bring the mixture up to just below the boiling point. It should thicken slightly.

Methods for Making a Reduction

1. Place the liquid in a heavy pot.
2. Bring it to a simmer and cook until the liquid has reduced to the desired consistency.
3. When reducing *au sec,* keep the heat very low near the end of cooking and watch the reduction carefully to prevent scorching.

How to Strain

- Conical sieves or chinois
- Cheesecloth (See Chapter 8, Sauces)

Miscellaneous Techniques

How to Prepare a Bain-Marie/Water Bath

1. Place a deep pan large enough to hold the baking dish comfortably on an oven rack. Add the baking dish. Place in the oven.
2. Pour in enough boiling water to come halfway to two-thirds of the way up the side of the dish.
3. Adjust the oven temperature as necessary to keep the water temperature between 180 and 190F° (82 and 88C°).

How to Cut Parchment Liners

1. Cut a square of parchment paper a little larger than the pan's diameter.
2. Fold the square in half to form a triangle.
3. Continue folding in half until a long triangle about an inch wide at its widest point is formed.
4. Position the triangle's narrow end above the pan's center and cut away the part that extends beyond the pan edge.

TOPIC: Beef, Veal, Lamb, Pork, and Game Fabrication

Cutting and Pounding Cutlets
Preparing Paillards
Preparing Émincé
Trimming a Tenderloin
Shaping Medallions
Tying a Roast
Cleaning a Skirt Steak
Frenching a Rack of Lamb
Cutting Steaks and Chops
Butterflying Meats
Trimming and Boning a Pork Loin
Boning a Leg of Veal
Working with Variety Meats
  Sweetbreads
  Liver
  Kidneys
  Tongue
  Removing Marrow

TOPIC: Poultry Fabrication

STANDARDS

The following standards must be adhered to strictly:

- Keep poultry under refrigeration when it is not being fabricated.
- Be sure that the cutting board has been thoroughly cleaned and sanitized before and after using it to cut up poultry.
- Clean and sanitize knives, poultry shears, and the steel before and after cutting poultry.
- Store poultry in clean, leak-proof containers, and do not place poultry above any cooked meats. If the poultry drips on the food below it, the food will become contaminated. For added safety, it may be a good idea to place a drip pan underneath the container holding the poultry.

- The essential tools for cutting up poultry are a clean work surface, a boning knife, and a chef's knife. Some chefs are comfortable using poultry shears to cut through joints and smaller bones.

Trussing Birds for Roasting Whole
Halving a Bird
   Removing the Keel Bone
   Preparing a Halved Bird to Grill or Broil
Quartering a Bird
Removing the Legs from a Whole Bird
Cutting a Bird in Eighths
Boneless, Skinless Chicken Breasts
Preparing Suprêmes
Boning a Poultry Leg
Disjointing a Rabbit

TOPIC: Fish and Shellfish Fabrication
   Gutting a Fish
   Scaling and Trimming Fish
   Pan-Dressed Fish
   Filleting a Fish
      Tranche
      Goujonette
      Paupiette
      Cutting Steaks
   Working with Shellfish
   Shrimp
      Peeling and Deveining Shrimp
      Butterflying Shrimp
   Lobster
      Working with Cooked Lobster
   Crayfish
   Crab
      Cleaning a Soft-Shelled Crab
   Mollusks
      Cleaning and Opening Clams and Oysters
      Cleaning and Debearding Mussels
   Cephalopods
      Cleaning Squid and Octopus
   Miscellaneous Items
      Cleaning a Sea Urchin
      Skinning an Eel
SUMMARY

Discussion Topics

TOPIC: Reminder of Knife Safety
- Handle knife with respect.
- Keep knives sharp.
- Keep knives clean.
- Use safe handling procedures for knives.
- Use an appropriate cutting surface.
- Keep knives properly stored.

Resource: Video

Knife Care: Selection, Sanitation and Safety. *Culinary Institute of America*, 1995.
Knife Skills: Vegetable Cuts. *Culinary Institute of America*, 1987.
Chicken Fabrication by the Professional Chef. *Culinary Institute of America*, 1996.
Fish Fabrication by the Professional Chef. *Culinary Institute of America*, 1996.

TOPIC: Establishing how much to prepare
- Par stock, which might change on a seasonal and daily basis
- Daily inventory
- Organizing your kitchen to fit your menu
  Determining how MUCH mise en place is necessary
  How many items from menu going to each station (even out workload or adjust to fit work ability of staff or station)

TOPIC: Mise en place organization
- Mental mise en place
- Daily assignments
- List posted with special prep assignments
- Daily inventory to check par stock, condition (use, discard, recycle)
- Using noncooking staff to help prep

TOPIC: Steps in mise en place
- Preparing raw ingredients
- Parcooking items
- Completely cooking some items

TOPIC: Contemporary spice blends (ethnic cuisine explored)

Resource: Books

Big Flavors of the Hot Sun: Hot Recipes and Cool Tips From the Spice Zone. Chris Schlesinger. Morrow. New York, 1994.

Spices: Roots & Fruit. Jill Norman. Bantam. New York, 1989.

TOPIC: Why do we marinate?
• To flavor
• To tenderize
• To preserve

TOPIC: Creating marinades
• Asian marinades: usually contain rice wine, soy sauce, sesame or peanut oil, typical Asian spices (star anise, Japanese 7-spice mix, Chinese 5-spice mix), lemongrass, gingerroot, bean paste, etc.
• Latin or South American marinades: might include citrus juice (lemon, lime, orange), papaya (which contains a natural tenderizer and is used in commercial meat tenderizing products), and aromatics, such as cilantro, cumin, chilis, and oregano
• European marinades: usually contain wine or beer, olive or vegetable oil, and herbs such as rosemary, thyme, parsley, oregano, sage, possibly mirepoix, etc.

TOPIC: Thickeners
• Types
• Applications
• Advantages
• Disadvantages

TOPIC: Stocks, Essences and Broths
• Made on premises vs. purchased/prepared
• Cost vs. quality
• Role in cooking

Additional material for this chapter may be found in the back of this manual. See "Knife Cuts," "Stocks," "Cooling Stocks," and "Marination."

Assignments

1   Saturday, the prep cook cut a case of potatoes for French fries. That night the restaurant got "slammed" and they ran out of prepped potatoes. Because French fries are a popular item in this family restaurant, they should not be taken off the menu. One of the cooks had to leave the line to prep another case of potatoes. This slowed the line down and many customers had to wait too long for their entrées. How could this have been avoided?
• The prep staff should prepare extra fries for a busy night. (With input from chef and manager of dining room.)
• Depending on the caliber of the restaurant, perhaps they could keep frozen French fries on hand for emergencies.
• In many restaurants, dishwashers assist with prep work and one could have been pulled off the dish machine.

2   For Labor Day weekend, the new entremetier prepared a gallon of gazpacho. He wasn't aware that the regular clientele went to the shore for the last weekend of the summer and business would be slow. On Monday, the soup was sour and the sous chef had to throw away half a gallon. What could the restaurant do to avoid this in the future?
• Par stock and mise en place should be reviewed and evaluated over holidays or other occasions that might affect business.
• It is also a good idea to review the reservation book from the previous year (if available) to see how business was.
• Input and direction from supervisor should be clearly communicated to new employees.

3   As the evening service period reaches its peak, some of the line cooks are having difficulty getting entrées and side dishes ready on time. Many menu items are not ready yet. Describe what they should have assembled as mise en place. Name as many items as you can. What could be done to avoid this in the future?
• A "mise en place for service" checklist should be prepared and posted as first prior-

ity activitiy (in conjunction with daily inventory)

Suggested mise en place:

- Soups cooked
- Sauces prepped or cooked, as applicable
- Vegetables, cut and parcooked, or cooked, as applicable
- Meats, poultry and fish—fabricated, possibly parcooked, smoked, roasted
- Salad, prepped
- Dressings for salad prepped
- Grains, beans cooked and in appropriate holding containers (e.g. in bain-marie or steam table)
- Potatoes cut, parcooked or cooked, as applicable
- Pasta prepped, and cooked in some cases
- Garnish items prepped and at correct temperature

4   Before he went on vacation, the chef ordered a boneless loin of pork from the purveyor. When it was delivered, the loin was bone-in. No one in the kitchen knew what to do, and eventually the loin of pork had to be thrown away. How could this have been handled? What can be done to avoid this in the future?

How to handle, e.g.:

- The loin could have been returned or exchanged.
- The loin could have been frozen until the chef returned.

In the future:

- Authorize someone on staff to return items for credit and alert purveyors.
- Train someone to cut meat.
- Leave reference books and recipes for the staff to use.

5   The stock prepared yesterday is pulled from the cooler to prepare a soup. The sous chef is suspicious that something might not be right. It seems cloudy and has a peculiar smell that becomes more intense as the stock is heated. What should the sous chef do?

- The sous chef should discard the stock.
- The sous chef should check how stock is

being prepared, cooled, and stored in the restaurant.

- If necessary, train staff again in all stages of proper preparation techniques.
- See also pages 249–253.

6   A restaurant has fried chicken on the menu, and it also serves many soups. The owner prefers to buy precut and prebreaded chicken and to purchase stock base for use in the soups. They also serve Buffalo wings as an appetizer. These, like the fried chicken, are purchased precut and precoated. One day, the accountant announces that there is simply not enough profit being made, and asks the owner to talk to the chef about ways to improve profit. What would you suggest?

- Buy whole or quartered chicken. Use the wings and thighs for Buffalo chicken wings. Use the breasts and legs for fried chicken and use any extra pieces to make stock. Extra wings and thighs might also be purchased. This total utilization will lower food cost, may increase labor cost, but should improve quality and, subsequently, sales.
- Build in a review process to evaluate whether or not savings are genuine.

7   The fish purveyor says that there is no lemon sole available today for the "Catch of the Day." However, there is a good buy on orange roughy. The chef isn't familiar with this fish, so she decides simply not to purchase any fish, even though "Catch of the Day" is a popular item on the menu. Explain what the consequences of her decision might be.

- Customers may be disappointed, especially if this is the only fish on the menu.
- The restaurant may lose customers.
- The chef should be willing to experiment with products that are new to her—even if she only ordered a small amount to begin with.
- Use purveyor as information resource regarding cooking technique.
- Absence of fish might have impact on other entrée availability as service period contin-

ues (i.e., customers who would have ordered fish all order chicken and now you have to "86" chicken also).

8 Discuss the benefits and drawbacks of using stocks and essences made on the premise versus purchased/prepared stocks and essences.

Stocks made on premises

Benefits: Better flavor
Better control of flavor
More versatility
Total utilization
Low food cost

Drawbacks: Labor intensive
Less consistency in quality
Storage/refrigeration space required

Prepared stocks

Benefits: Consistency
Less labor involved
Less storage/refrigeration space required
Convenience

Drawbacks: Waste of trim and otherwise wholesome but unsaleable foods
Higher food cost
Flavor

Answer Key to Self-Study Questions

1 (a) Racks or chops of lamb, veal, or pork; wing bones of a poultry suprême.

(b) To french a rack, cut the fat covering away about 3 inches above the eye of the meat, then make slits between each bone. On the other side, score the membrane covering the bones, then push the bones through the membranes using opposing force between thumbs and forefingers. Finally, cut away the meat surrounding the bone ends and trim the fat.

For chops or poultry bones, scrape in a downward motion to remove meat, skin, and tendons.

2 "To put in place." A state of readiness.

3 (1) Grasp the handle with the thumb over the spine of the blade.
(2) Grasp the handle with the thumb along side the blade.
(3) Grasp the handle with the thumb and two fingers along either side of the blade. Delicate cutting or shaping calls for greater control. Coarser chopping and cutting tasks require a firmer grip and more leverage.

4 (a) Guiding hand is the hand not holding the knife.
(b) It is used to hold in place the object that is being cut.

5 • Fine julienne—$1/16 \times 1/16 \times 1$ to 2 inches
• Julienne / Allumette—$1/8 \times 1/8 \times 1$ to 2 inches
• Bâtonnet—$1/4 \times 1/4 \times 2$ to $2 1/2$ inches
• Brunoise—$1/8 \times 1/8 \times 1/8$ inch
• Small dice—$1/4 \times 1/4 \times 1/4$ inch
• Medium dice—$1/2 \times 1/2 \times 1/2$ inch
• Large dice—$3/4 \times 3/4 \times 3/4$ inch
• Paysanne—$1/2 \times 1/2 \times 1/8$ inch
• Tourné—seven 2-inch sides
• Coarse chopping, mincing and chiffonade—no dimensions

6 • Fluting—done with mushrooms
• Fanning—done with numerous pliable foods, such as pickles, strawberries, peach halves, zucchini, avocado, etc.
• Tourné—done with firm, round vegetables, such as potatoes or carrots
• Oblique or roll cut—done with long, cylindrical vegetables, such as parsnips, carrots, and celery

7 (1) Trim.
(2) Split in half lengthwise.
(3) Rinse under running water until there is no trace of dirt remaining.

8 (1) Cut an "X" in the bottom of the tomato.
(2) Immerse in boiling water for up to 30 seconds; remove and plunge in ice water immediately, then pull away the skin.
(3) Halve, squeeze out the seeds.
(4) Cut or chop as needed.

9 (1) Char small quantities by holding over an open flame or placing on a grill.

(2) Oven- or broiler-roast large quantities on a sheet pan in a very hot oven or under a broiler.

Peppers may also be blistered by deep-frying.

10 (1) Plunge the separated leaves or loosened heads of greens in and out of a sink filled with cool water to loosen the sand.

(2) Lift the greens out, check the water for traces of grit, then repeat the process as many times as necessary until no grit remains.

(3) Drain the greens, or spin them dry.

11 (1) Place rinsed and sorted beans in a container and cover them with cool water.

(2) Let the beans soak for anywhere from 4 to 24 hours, depending on the type of bean.

(3) Drain the beans and cook as directed.

12 • Slurries—made with arrowroot, cornstarch, or rice flour mixed with cool liquid

• Beurre manié—mixture of equal amounts of softened whole butter and flour

• Roux—a cooked mixture of equal amounts of fat (butter, chicken fat, vegetable oil, rendered fat from roasts) and flour

• Liaison—a mixture of egg yolks and cream

• Gelatin—sheets or crystals of processed animal protein "bloomed" in cool water, dissolved over light heat, combined with liquid preparations, then chilled to set

13 • Bouquet garni is a combination of fresh vegetables and herbs, typically including celery stalk, parsley stems, thyme, and a bay leaf, tied into a bundle.

• Sachet d'epices does not contain a vegetable (no celery stalk), and adds to the above herbs, cracked black peppercorns, all tied together in a cheesecloth bag.

14 • Oil and acid

• Oil and aromatics

• Acid and aromatics

• Dry marinades and rubs

15 Mixture of finely chopped and sautéed mushrooms, shallots, parsley, and sometimes white wine that is cooked until almost all of the moisture has evaporated. Used as a flavoring, stuffing, or coating.

16 • Neutral stock—white beef stock

• Fumet—essence, prepared by sweating fish bones with vegetables and simmering together in water and white wine

• Court bouillon—short broth, prepared as the cooking liquid for fish or vegetables, and composed of aromatic vegetables, herbs, water, and an acid

• Remouillage—a rewetting of bones that have already been used to make a primary stock

• Estouffade—a brown stock prepared by simmering together meaty veal bones, pork, vegetables, and other aromatics

17 • Beef stock—8 pounds bones to 6 quarts water to 1 pound mirepoix and a sachet d'epices or bouquet garni per gallon, cooked for 6 to 8 hours

• Veal stock—same as above

• Poultry stock—ratio of ingredients same as above; cooking time 3 hours

• Fish fumet—11 pounds bones to 5 quarts water to 1 pound mirepoix and a sachet d'epices or bouquet garni per gallon, cooked for 30 minutes to 1 hour

18 • Blanched to remove any impurities that may be present.

• Bones are placed in a pot, covered with cool water, brought to a full boil, skimmed, drained, and rinsed.

• Browned to begin the process of flavor development. Bones are rinsed, if necessary, and dried, added in an even layer to a preheated roasting pan, and roasted to a rich brown color. Mirepoix and tomato product may be added with bones or after they are removed. Placed in a stockpot to begin stock pack process. Roasting pan is deglazed and added to stock.

19 (a) Cool by straining into a clean metal container, placing the container in a cool water bath, stirring the stock until temperature of 40°F (4°C) is reached.

(b) Store cooled stocks in storage containers, sealed, and labeled, with the contents and date, place in a walk-in or reach-in.

20 • Butter heated to separate out milk solids and other impurities; pure butterfat.
   • Ghee is clarified butter that has been simmered longer to highly clarify the butterfat.

21 • Use a copper bowl for whipping.
   • Be sure that all traces of fat have been removed by rinsing bowls and whips with white vinegar and then rinsing well with hot water.
   • Egg whites should be allowed to come to room temperature before whipping.

22 • Soft meringue—whipping egg whites with granulated sugar
   • Swiss (hard) meringue—whipping egg whites with an even greater proportion of sugar
   • Italian meringue—whipping egg whites with a sugar syrup

23 (a) To keep the yolks from scrambling, thus producing a smoother finished product
   (b) Hot liquid is gradually added, whipping constantly until the temperature of the liaison has risen to near the temperature of the appareil; mixture is gradually whipped back into the remaining appareil; cooked until appropriately thickened.

24 (a) Thin boneless cut taken from a tender part of the animal, such as the loin, tenderloin, or top round
   (b) Pounded to an even thickness for rapid sautéing or pan-frying

25 • To ensure even cooking
   • To help the roast retain its shape after roasting

26 (a) Thymus gland of young animals
   (b) They must be soaked in cool water to remove all traces of blood, blanched in a court bouillon to loosen the outer membrane, which is then peeled away and discarded; they are then pressed to give them a firmer, more appealing texture.

27 • Keep poultry iced and under refrigeration when not being fabricated or cooked

• Clean and sanitize the cutting board before and after using
• Clean and sanitize knives and any other equipment
• Store poultry in clean, leak-proof containers below any cooked meats in a walk-in or reach-in

28 (a) Semi-boneless poultry breast
   (b) Cut the breast away from the rib cage, then cut away the wing tips, leaving one section still attached; then french the bone.

29 (a) As soon as possible after being caught.
   (b) Round fish: make a slit in belly and pull out viscera (guts); rinse well.
   (c) Flat fish: cut a notch from fin near head to outside of fish, insert thumb behind eyes, pull head and viscera (guts) away, rinse well.

30 Single-portion fish that have been scaled, gutted and trimmed; in some cases, the head and tail are also removed; most often pan-fried or grilled.

31 • Tranche—an angled slice from the fillet
   • Goujonette—small strips, often breaded or dipped in batter and deep-fried
   • Paupiette—a thin, rolled fillet (may be filled with forcemeat or stuffing) shallow-poached
   • Steaks—cross-cuts of the fish

32 (1) Debeard.
   (2) Scrub under running water to remove all dirt.
   (3) Check carefully for tightly closed shells; any that are open, or that feel heavy are either dead or close to death and should be discarded, (as is true for all mollusks).

33 Insert the tip of a knife into the back of the lobster, just behind the head, which severs the spinal nerve.

Keywords

Allumette: Vegetables, potatoes, or other items cut into pieces the size and shape of match sticks, $\frac{1}{8}$ inch × $\frac{1}{8}$ inch × 1 to 2 inches is the standard.

Appareil: A prepared mixture of ingredients used alone or as an ingredient in another preparation.

Bâton/Bâtonnet (Fr.): Items cut into pieces somewhat larger than allumette or julienne; ¼ inch × ¼ inch × 2 to 3 inches is the standard. Translated to English as "stick" or "small stick."

Beurre manié (Fr.): "Kneaded butter." A mixture of equal parts by weight of whole butter and flour, used to thicken gravies and sauces.

Bouquet garni: A small bundle of herbs tied with string. It is used to flavor stocks, braises, and other preparations. Usually contains bay leaf, parsley, thyme, and possibly other aromatics.

Broth: A flavorful, aromatic liquid made by simmering water or stock with meat, vegetables, and/or spices and herbs.

Brunoise (Fr.): Small dice; ¼-inch square is the standard. For a brunoise cut, items are first cut in julienne, then cut crosswise. For a fine brunoise, ⅛-inch square, cut items first in fine julienne.

Butterfly: To cut an item (usually meat or seafood) and open out the edges like a book or the wings of a butterfly.

Chiffonade: Leafy vegetables or herbs cut into fine shreds; often used as a garnish.

Clarification; clarifying: The process of removing solid impurities from a liquid (such as butter or stock). Also, a mixture of ground meat, egg whites, mirepoix, tomato purée, herbs, and spices used to clarify broth for consommé.

Coarse chop: To cut into pieces of roughly the same size; used for items such as mirepoix, where appearance is not important.

Court bouillon (Fr.): "Short broth." An aromatic vegetable broth that usually includes an acidic ingredient, such as wine or vinegar; most commonly used for poaching fish.

Cutlet: A meat cut made from a boneless piece of meat; usually cut against the grain. May be pounded if necessary or desired.

Diagonal cut: Foods cut on the bias to expose more of their interior.

Dice: To cut ingredients into small cubes (¼ inch for small, ½ inch for medium, ¾ inch for large standard).

Emincé (Fr.): To cut an item, usually meat, into very thin slices.

Estouffade (Fr.): Stew. Also, a type of brown stock based on pork knuckle and veal and beef bones that is often used in braises.

Fermière (farmer's style): A knife cut that results in foods cut into a tile shape.

Fillet/Filet: A boneless cut of meat, fish, or poultry.

Fine brunoise: ⅛-inch square. See BRUNOISE.

Frenching: The process of scraping meat from bones before cooking.

Fumet (Fr.); (essence): A type of stock in which the main flavoring ingredient is allowed to smother with wine and aromatics; fish fumet is the most common type.

Goujonettes (Fr.): Fish fillet cut in strips and usually breaded or batter coated and then deep-fried.

Julienne: Vegetables, potatoes, or other items cut into thin strips; ⅛-inch square × 1 to 2 inches is standard. Fine julienne is ¹⁄₁₆-inch square × 1 to 2 inches.

Liaison: A mixture of egg yolks and cream used to thicken and enrich sauces. (Also loosely applied to any appareil used as a thickener.)

Lozenge (diamond cut): A knife cut in which foods are cut into small diamond shapes.

Marinade: An appareil used before cooking to flavor and moisten foods; may be liquid or dry. Liquid marinades are usually based on an acidic ingredient, such as wine or vinegar; dry marinades are usually salt based.

Marrow: The substance found in the interior of bones. May be used as a garnish in sauces.

Matignon (Fr.): An edible mirepoix that is often used in poêléed dishes and is usually served with the finished dish. Typically, matignon includes two parts carrot, one part celery, one part leek, one part onion, one part mushroom (optional), and one part ham or bacon.

Medallion (Fr.): A small, round scallop of meat.

Mie de pain (Fr.): The soft part of bread (not the crust); mie de pain is fresh white bread crumbs.

Mince/mincing: To chop into very small pieces.

Mirepoix: A combination of chopped aromatic vegetables—usually two parts onion, one part carrot, and one part celery—used to flavor stocks, soups, braises, and stews.

Oblique (roll cut): A knife cut used primarily with long, cylindrical vegetables such as carrots. The item is cut on a diagonal, rolled 180 degrees, then cut on the same diagonal, producing a piece with two angled edges.

Oignon brûlé (Fr.): "Burnt onion." A peeled, halved onion seared on a flat-top or in a skillet and used to enhance the color of stock and consommé.

Oignon piqué (Fr.): "Pricked onion." A whole, peeled onion to which a bay leaf is attached, using a whole clove as a tack. It is used to flavor béchamel sauce and some soups.

Paillard (Fr.): A scallop of meat pounded until thin; usually grilled.

Pan-dressed: A portion-sized fish that has been gutted, scaled, trimmed of fins (the head and tail may be left on or removed, as desired) before cooking.

Paupiette: A fillet or scallop of fish or meat that is rolled up around a stuffing and poached or braised.

Paysanne cut (peasant-style): A knife cut in which ingredients are cut into flat, square pieces, ½ inch by ½ inch by ⅛ inch is standard.

Remouillage (Fr.): "Re-wetting." A stock made from bones that have already been used for stock; it is weaker than a first-quality stock and is often reduced to make glaze.

Render: To melt fat and clarify the drippings for use in sautéing or pan-frying.

Rondelle (rounds): A knife cut that produces flat, round or oval pieces; used on cylindrical vegetables or items trimmed into cylinders before cutting.

Roux (Fr.): An appareil containing equal parts of flour and fat (usually butter) used to thicken liquids. Roux is cooked to varying degrees (white, pale/blond, or brown), depending on its intended use.

Sachet d'épices (Fr.): "Bag of spices." Aromatic ingredients, encased in cheesecloth, that are used to flavor stocks and other liquids. A standard sachet contains parsley stems, cracked peppercorns, dried thyme, and a bay leaf.

Slurry: Starch dispersed in cold liquid to prevent it from forming lumps when added to hot liquid as a thickener.

Steak: A portion-size (or larger) cut of meat, poultry, or fish made by cutting across the grain of a muscle or a muscle group. May be boneless or bone-in.

Stock: A flavorful liquid prepared by simmering meat, poultry, seafood, and/or vegetables in water with aromatics until their flavor is extracted. It is used as a base for soups, sauces, and other preparations.

Suprême (Fr.): The breast fillet and wing of chicken or other poultry. Sauce suprême is chicken velouté enriched with cream.

Temper: To heat gently and gradually. May refer to the process of incorporating hot liquid into a liaison to gradually raise its temperature. May also refer to the proper method for melting chocolate.

Tomato concassé: A tomato that has been peeled, seeded, and chopped.

Tourner/Tourné: To cut items, usually vegetables, into barrel, olive, or football shapes.

Tranche (Fr.): A slice or cut of meat, fish, or poultry.

Truss/trussing: To tie up meat or poultry with string before cooking it in order to give it a compact shape for more even cooking and better appearance.

Soups

Objectives

- Describe the basic techniques for preparing the following kinds of soup:
    Broths (pages 297–299)
    Consommés (pages 299–302)
    Clear vegetable soups (pages 302–303)
    Cream and velouté soups (pages 303–306)
    Purée soups (pages 306–308)
    Bisques (pages 308–310)
    Special soups (page 310)
    Cold soups (page 310)
- Identify quality products used to make soup and the standards used to assess a soup's overall quality (interspersed throughout chapter)
- Understand how to select an appropriate garnish for a soup and how to properly heat it (page 311)
- Describe the soup service guidelines (page 310)
- Apply the proper cooling, storing, and reheating procedures for all types of soup (page 311)

Lecture Outline

TYPES OF SOUPS
- Broths
- Consommés
- Clear Vegetable Soups
- Cream Soups and Velouté Soups
- Purée Soups
- Bisques
- Special Soups (including international and regional)
- Cold Soups

BASIC SOUP-MAKING TECHNIQUES
Broths
- Proper selection of ingredients
- Careful monitoring of the broth as it develops
- Safe handling procedures throughout cooking, cooling, reheating, and service

Mise en Place
1. Assemble all ingredients necessary for making the broth.
2. Assemble all necessary equipment for preparing broth.

Method

1. Combine the principle ingredients with a cool liquid and bring the broth to a gentle boil.
2. Add the remaining ingredients at appropriate intervals.
3. Check the flavor of the broth periodically during cooking time.
4. Strain the broth carefully through a fine sieve or bouillon strainer.

Consommé

- Full flavor
- Rich, noticeable body
- A succulence and savor that last in the mouth
- A deep amber to brown color
- Clarity
- Well-balanced flavor

Mise en Place

1. Assemble the ingredients and appareils necessary for the consommé.
2. Assemble all necessary equipment for preparing consommés.

Method

1. Blend the ingredients for the clarification and add the broth.
2. Bring the consommé slowly to a boil.
3. Once the raft forms, establish a gentle, even simmer.
4. Continue to simmer the consommé until it has fully developed.
5. Strain the finished consommé carefully. It is now ready for either service or to be properly cooled and stored.

Sidebar *Fixing a Cloudy Consommé*

Clear Vegetable Soups

Mise en Place

1. Assemble and prepare all ingredients and appareils necessary.
2. Assemble all equipment necessary for cooking.

Method

1. Sweat the aromatic vegetables.
2. Add the stock, broth, or water and bring the soup slowly to a boil.

3. Add any remaining ingredients at appropriate intervals.
4. Cook until all ingredients are fully cooked and tender and the soup's flavor is developed.
5. The soup is now ready for final seasoning, garnishing, and service. Or, it may be properly cooled and stored.

Cream Soups and Velouté Soups

Mise en Place

1. Assemble and prepare all ingredients and appareils necessary.
2. Assemble all equipment necessary for cooking.

Method

1. Sweat the aromatic vegetables.
2. Add the liquid base for the soup, and bring it to a gentle simmer.
3. Add the additional ingredients at appropriate intervals.
4. Simmer the soup gently until it has developed the appropriate flavor, body, and texture.
5. Strain the solids from the soup.
6. The soup is now ready to be finished, seasoned, and garnished, or it may be properly cooled and stored.

Purée Soups

Mise en Place

1. Assemble and prepare the ingredients.
2. Assemble all equipment necessary for cooking.

Method

1. Sweat the aromatic vegetables.
2. Add the liquid and any additional ingredients required at this point. Bring the soup to a gentle simmer.
3. Add additional ingredients at the correct point and continue to simmer until all the ingredients are soft enough to purée easily.
4. Purée the soup.
5. The soup is now ready to garnish and serve, or it may be properly cooled and stored.

Bisques

  Mise en Place

    1. Assemble and prepare all ingredients.

    2. Assemble all equipment necessary for cooking.

  Method

    1. Sear the shells in oil or clarified butter.

    2. Add the aromatic vegetables and allow them to sweat.

    3. Add the tomato paste and cook until it takes on a deep rust color.

    4. Add the brandy and cook it out.

    5. Add the liquid and additional appropriate ingredients and bring the soup to a simmer.

    6. Simmer the bisque until it is well flavored and has a good consistency.

    7. Strain and purée the soup.

    8. The bisque is now ready to garnish and serve, or it may be cooled and properly stored.

  Special Soups

  Cold Soups

SOUP SERVICE GUIDELINES

  Reheating Soups

  Final Seasoning and Consistency Adjustments

  Garnishes

SUMMARY

Discussion Topics

TOPIC: Roles of soup on menu
- Meal
- Appetizer
- Soup tasting (offer sampling of three)

TOPIC: Contemporary soup ideas, e.g.:
- Autumn Squash Apple Cider Soup
- Chilled Red Plum Soup
- Chilled Apple Soup
- Beet Fennel Ginger Soup
- Others

Resource: Magazines

Food and Wine
Food Arts
Chef
Saveur

TOPIC: Ways to vary classic soups to make them more contemporary
- Lighter versions of cream soups
- Modify garniture

Resource: Magazines

Eating Well, including "Rx for Recipes," bimonthly feature
Cooking Light

Resource: Book

Techniques of Healthy Cooking. Culinary Institute of America. Mary Donovan, ed. Van Nostrand Reinhold. New York, 1993.

TOPIC: Regional soups, e.g.:
- Corn Chowder
- Gumbo
- Maryland Crab Soup
- Peanut Soup
- Philadelphia Pepper Pot Soup
- Chili
- Sweet Potato Soup
- Pumpkin Soup
- Amish-Style Chicken Corn Soup
- New England-Style Clam Chowder

TOPIC: International soups, e.g.:
- French Lentil Soup
- Bergen Fish Soup
- Billi Bi Soup (mussels in a fish velouté base)
- Budnersuppe (barley with air-dried beef)
- Cock-a-Leekie (hens and prunes)
- Finnish Salmon Soup
- Hungarian Goulash Soup
- Erwtensoep (green split pea soup)
- Menudo (tripe)

- Oxtail Soup à l'Anglaise
- Caldo Verde (potato kale soup)
- Velouté Dieppoise (mussels and shrimp in a velouté base)
- Waterzooi de Poulet (chicken velouté soup)
- Chinese Hot and Sour Soup

TOPIC: Soup service setup
- Cold soups
- Steam table or warmer
- Garnishes, hot and cold
- Waiters' role in service
- Reheating

TOPIC: Pairing soups with fixed-price or banquet menu items
- No cream soup with cream sauce entrée
- Light broth with heavy entree
- Hot soup with cold appetizer
- No fish soup if serving fish course

Additional material for this chapter may be found in the back of this manual. See "Consommé Clarification," "How to Incorporate Roux," and "Convection Diagram."

Assignments

1 At the Soup Kitchen Cafe, it is a very busy day and several of the staff called in sick. Because of this, several things have gone wrong. For each of the following problems (A-E), explain what might have happened, if it can be corrected, and how it could be avoided in the future.
   A. The sherried chicken soup was prepared and put in a bain-marie on the steam table. Halfway through service time it developed a bad flavor and color.
      - The heat from the steam table will cook the sherry and it will taste bad.
      - For delicate soups it is often best to keep most of it under refrigeration and heat only a small portion at a time. This portion can then be held in the bain-marie.

Also, in this case, it would be best to add the sherry in small portions, just prior to service.
      - Discard batch and reheat smaller, fresh batches or individual portions "to order."
      - See also pages 310–311.
   B. The croutons for the soup were made three days ago. They were placed in a steam table insert, covered with plastic and kept on a shelf over the stove. Today, the customers complain that the croutons are stale.
      - The heat and moisture from the stove will turn the covered croutons soft.
      - When possible, it is best to make croutons daily. They should be covered and held in a dry, cool, environment, not over the stove.
      - Try putting croutons on a sheet tray and heat/dry/toast quickly in conventional or convection oven.
      - See also page 237.
   C. Even after clarification, the consommé is cloudy.
      - Clarification was not done correctly.
      - Repeat the process of clarification using just the egg white. Add a few more vegetables for flavor, if desired.
      - If possible, remove consommé from menu and replace with vegetable soup made by adding vegetable garnish directly to consommé.
      - Teach the employee how to do it correctly.
      - See also pages 299–302.
   D. The cream soup is very thick, with a starchy and almost-scorched flavor.
      - The soup was cooked too long over low heat, or in a thin pan over too-high heat.
      - Thin soup with broth or water, readjust seasoning and taste again, to see if it can be served.
      - Consider adding a garnish with a "smoky" flavor (roasted or smoked meats, vegetables, chipotles), or a strong flavor (pesto, grated cheese, herbs, or spices) if scorched taste is not too strong.

- Discard, if scorched flavor is still apparent.
- See also page 303–306.

E. The cucumber-yogurt soup was so thick you could stand up a spoon in it.

  - The soup should be thinned with buttermilk, milk, or cream. Or, to highlight cucumber flavor, add puréed cucumbers. (Remember to adjust seasoning after thinning).

2 Soups provide an opportunity for total utilization of ingredients required for other menu items. Discuss the ways in which a chef can be creative with soups to reduce waste and overall food cost and increase profit.

  - Soups may contain the wholesome edible portions of meat, poultry, and fish that are not used for other items.
  - Wholesome vegetable trimmings may be used, especially for purées.
  - Unused wholesome cooked vegetables, beans, grains, rice, and pasta may be added to soups at service time.
  - Daily soup specials.
  - See also page 310.

Answer Key to Self-Study Questions

1 Clarification is the removal of any solid impurities suspended in a liquid to produce a completely clear product. Proteins and acids present in clarification are beaten and then coagulate, trapping impurities into a solid mass referred to as a raft.

  (1) Blend the ingredients for the clarification, then add cold broth and stir to combine.
  (2) Bring the consommé slowly to a boil, stirring constantly until the raft begins to form.
  (3) Stop stirring and establish a gentle simmer.
  (4) Continue simmering until the consommé's flavor is fully developed and the raft begins to sink slightly.

  (5) Carefully strain the consommé.
  (6) Serve very hot with an appropriate garnish.

2 Slightly thicker than heavy cream; it should not be so thick that a spoon is able to stand upright in it.

3 Stock is a foundation ingredient used in other preparation, not intended for service on its own, and is based on bones. Broth is flavorful enough to be served "as is", it is usually made with pieces of meat or large quantities of vegetables.

4 Bisques are traditionally based on crustaceans, classically thickened with rice. Cream soups can be based on a velouté or béchamel and major flavoring ingredient allowed to simmer in base.

5
  - Roux—whisked into the base liquid
  - Liaison—generally tempered into the soup toward the end of the cooking time
  - A purée of starchy ingredients—cooked in a soup and later puréed in part or in total to provide body and thickness

6
  - Crystal-clear
  - No visible droplets of fat floating on its surface
  - Deep amber to brown in color
  - Substantial, well-balanced flavor and body
  - Served hot with an appropriate garnish

7
  - Hot soups should be hot, served in heated dishes
  - Cold soups should be cold, served in chilled dishes
  - Appropriate garnishes should be at the correct temperature
  - Plate just before pick-up
  - Rims of bowls and any liner plates should be clean, with no splatters or spills

8
  - No larger than the size of the spoon, or soft enough to be cut through with a spoon
  - Should not be difficult to eat
  - Should not overwhelm the soup cup or plate

9
  - Royales
  - Quenelles
  - Neatly diced and perfectly cooked root vegetables

- Chopped fresh herbs
- Crêpes (cut into shreds)
- Wontons
- Gnocchi
- Gold leaves

10 (a) Stewing hen
   (b) Has a deeper, more savory flavor than a younger hen

11 • Raft begins to sink
   - Color becomes dark and lustrous
   - Aroma is rich
   - Flavor deepens and body becomes noticeable

Keywords

Bisque: A soup based on crustaceans or a vegetable purée. It is classically thickened with rice and usually finished with cream.

Broth: A flavorful, aromatic liquid made by simmering water or stock with meat, vegetables, and/or spices and herbs.

Chowder: A thick soup that may be made from a variety of ingredients but usually contains potatoes.

Clarification; clarifying: The process of removing solid impurities from a liquid (such as butter or stock). Also, a mixture of ground meat, egg whites, mirepoix, tomato purée, herbs, and spices used to clarify broth for consommé.

Consommé: Broth that has been clarified using a mixture of ground meat, egg whites, and other ingredients that traps impurities.

Cream soup: Traditionally a soup based on a béchamel sauce. Loosely, any soup finished with cream, a cream variant such as sour cream, or a liaison; these soups are usually based on béchamel or velouté.

Garbure (Fr.): A thick vegetable soup usually containing beans, cabbage, and/or potatoes.

Garnish: An edible decoration or accompaniment to a dish.

Gazpacho (Sp.): A cold soup made from vegetables, typically tomatoes, cucumbers, peppers, and onions.

Gumbo: A Creole soup/stew thickened with filé or okra.

Minestrone: A vegetable soup, typically includes dried beans and pasta.

Pincé/pinçage (Fr.): To caramelize an item by sautéing; usually refers to a tomato product.

Pot au feu (Fr.): A classic French boiled dinner that typically includes poultry and beef, along with various root vegetables. The broth is often served as a first course, followed by the meats and vegetables.

Purée soup: A soup made by cooking various ingredients in a broth or other liquid until tender enough to purée. Typically, the base ingredients provide all the necessary thickening.

Raft: A mixture of ingredients used to clarify consommé (see CLARIFICATION). The term refers to the fact that the ingredients rise to the surface and form a floating mass.

Sear: To brown the surface of food in fat over high heat before finishing by another method (for example, braising) in order to add flavor.

Temper: To heat gently and gradually. May refer to the process of incorporating hot liquid into a liaison to gradually raise its temperature. May also refer to the proper method for melting chocolate.

Vegetable soup: A broth- or water-based soup garnished primarily with vegetables; may include meats, legumes, and noodles as well; may be clear or thick.

Velouté soup: A cream soup made with a velouté sauce base and flavorings (usually puréed) that is usually finished with a liaison.

CHAPTER 8

Sauces

Objectives

- Explain the function of a sauce in relation to the other components of a dish (page 316)
- Select a suitable sauce for the style of service and the cooking technique applied to the main ingredient (page 317)
- Name all the grand sauces and derivatives for each (interspersed throughout chapter)
- Identify some contemporary and miscellaneous sauces (pages 317 and 339)
- Describe and outline the techniques used to make sauces (interspersed throughout chapter)
- Explain how sauces are properly reheated, held, and plated (pages 339–340)

Lecture Outline

POINTS TO CONSIDER WHEN SELECTING THE APPROPRIATE SAUCE:

- The sauce should be suitable for the style of service.
- The sauce should be suitable for the main ingredient's cooking technique.
- The sauce's flavor should be appropriate for the flavor of the food with which it is paired.

THE GRAND SAUCES

CONTEMPORARY SAUCES

- They usually take less time to prepare.
- They are more likely to be specifically tailored to a given food or technique.
- They have a lighter color, texture, and flavor than some of the grand sauces.
- They are more likely to be thickened and fin-

ished using emulsions, modified starches, or reduction and less likely to contain roux.

TECHNIQUES FOR CLASSIC AND CONTEMPORARY SAUCES

Brown Sauce (Sauce Espagnole)

Mise en Place

1. Assemble the ingredients and preparations necessary to prepare brown sauce.
   - Brown veal stock or estouffade
   - Mirepoix, cut into large dice
   - Tomato purée
   - Brown roux
2. Assemble and prepare the equipment necessary for preparing brown sauce.

Method

1. Sweat the mirepoix in a little oil or clarified butter until juices are released and onions are translucent.

2. Add the tomato purée and sauté until caramelized.
3. Add brown stock to the mirepoix, bring it to a boil, and gradually incorporate the brown roux.
4. Simmer the sauce for approximately 2 to 3 hours, skimming the surface throughout the cooking time.
5. Strain the sauce through a sieve. At this point, the sauce is ready for use in other preparations, or it may be properly cooled and stored for later use.

Demi-Glace
  Mise en Place
    1. Assemble the ingredients and preparations necessary for demi-glace.
      • Brown veal stock or estouffade
      • Brown sauce
    2. Assemble the equipment necessary for preparing demi-glace.
  Method
    1. Combine equal parts of the brown veal stock and sauce espagnole in a heavy-bottomed pot and bring to a boil, then reduce the heat slightly to maintain a simmer.
    2. Simmer until the sauce is reduced to half its original volume.
    3. Strain, using either the wringing or milking techniques.

Preparing Demi-Glace Derivatives
  • Finishing with a fortified wine
  • Reduction
  • Finishing with butter (monté au beurre)

Jus Lié
  Mise en Place
    1. Assemble the ingredients and preparations necessary to prepare jus lié.
      • Brown stock
      • Mirepoix, cut into large dice
      • Tomato purée
      • Arrowroot, diluted in a cold liquid
    2. Assemble and prepare the equipment necessary for preparing jus lié.

Method
    1. Sweat the mirepoix in a little oil or clarified butter until juices are released and onions are golden.
    2. Add the tomato purée and sauté until caramelized.
    3. Add brown stock to the mirepoix, bring it to a boil, and simmer over low heat for about 4 to 6 hours.
    4. Add the slurry to the simmering sauce, and continue to cook another 2 to 3 minutes.
    5. Strain the sauce through a sieve.

Velouté
  Mise en Place
    1. Assemble the necessary ingredients and preparations to prepare velouté.
      • White stock (veal, chicken, fish, or vegetable)
      • Pale roux
      • Optional seasoning or flavoring ingredients as desired
    2. Assemble the necessary equipment to prepare velouté.
  Method
    1. Bring the stock to a simmer. Gradually whip in the roux.
    2. Bring to a full boil, then reduce the heat to establish a simmer.
    3. Strain the sauce through a fine sieve.
    4. The sauce is now ready to be served or it may be properly cooled and stored for later use.

Béchamel
  Mise en Place
    1. Assemble the ingredients and preparations necessary for béchamel.
      • Milk
      • White roux, prepared with oil
      • Aromatics
    2. Assemble the equipment necessary to prepare béchamel.
  Method
    1. Sweat the minced onion in a small amount of oil.

2. Add the flour to the onion and prepare a white roux.
3. Gradually add the milk to the roux and bring the sauce to a simmer.
4. Add the grated nutmeg to taste before straining the sauce.
5. The sauce is now ready for service, or it may be cooled and stored properly.

Tomato Sauce
  Mise en Place
    1. Assemble the ingredients and preparations necessary for tomato sauce.
       • Plum tomatoes (fresh or canned)
       • Tomato purée (fresh or canned)
       • Ground salt pork, oil, or clarified butter
       • Stock: veal, chicken, beef, pork, or vegetable, as desired
       • Aromatic vegetables, cut into a medium dice
       • Sachet d'épices or bouquet garni
       • Additional or optional flavoring or seasoning items
    2. Assemble the equipment necessary for preparing tomato sauce.
  Method
    1. Heat the oil, butter, or ground salt pork in a pot over low heat. Then, add the aromatic vegetables and allow them to sweat.
    2. Add the remaining ingredients and bring to a simmer.
    3. Simmer the sauce until the flavor is fully developed, and strain.
    4. Purée the sauce through a food mill fitted with a fine disk.
    5. The sauce is ready to serve now or it may be properly cooled and stored.

Coulis
Hollandaise
  Mise en Place
    1. Assemble the ingredients and preparations necessary for hollandaise.
       • Unsalted butter, melted or clarified, and warm
       • Egg yolks
       • Reduction
       • Water
       • Fresh lemon juice
       • Additional or optional seasoning, flavoring, or garnish ingredients
    2. Assemble all equipment necessary to prepare a hollandaise.
  Method
    1. Make the reduction and add a small amount of water to cool it. Transfer the reduction (strained, if desired) to a stainless steel bowl.
    2. Add egg yolks to the reduction and whip over barely simmering water until they are thickened and frothy.
    3. Add warm butter gradually in a thin stream, whipping constantly. Season to taste as desired.
    4. The sauce is now ready to serve. Keep it warm (at around 160°F/70°C).

Sidebar Special Tips to Rescue a Broken Hollandaise
Beurre Blanc
  Mise en Place
    1. Assemble the ingredients and preparations necessary for beurre blanc.
       • Whole unsalted butter, diced and chilled
       • Reduction
       • Reduced heavy cream (optional)
       • Additional seasoning, flavoring, or garnish ingredients
    2. Assemble all equipment necessary to prepare a beurre blanc.
  Method
    1. Make the reduction and add a small amount of cream, if desired.
    2. Add chilled diced butter to the reduction and incorporate over low heat until the sauce is the correct consistency.
    3. The sauce is now ready to serve. Keep it warm (at around 160°F/70°C).

Sauce Vin Blanc
  Method 1 for Sauce Vin Blanc
  Method 2 for Sauce Vin Blanc
  Method 3 for Sauce Vin Blanc

Compound Butter
  Mise en Place
  - Whole unsalted butter
  - The desired flavoring ingredients
  Method
  1. Prepare the flavoring agents or according to individual recipes.
  2. Incorporate the flavoring agents into the softened butter by hand with a spoon, or with a mixer or food processor.
  3. Roll the butter into a cylinder in parchment paper or pipe it into individual rosettes. Thoroughly chill the butter before service.

MISCELLANEOUS SAUCES
- Broths, essences, and juices
- Pilafs, risottos, ragouts, and stews
- Barbecue sauces and glazes
- Compotes, marmalades, conserves, and chutneys
- Salsas and other "raw sauces"
- Cold emulsion sauces (mayonnaise, vinaigrettes, and marinades)
- Infused oils

SERVING SAUCES
  Reheating Sauces
  Holding a Finished Sauce
  Plating and Presentation
  SUMMARY

Discussion Topics

TOPIC: Contemporary Sauces
- Compare with the grand sauces
- "Classic" contemporary sauce—jus lié, beurre blanc, coulis
- Salsas, chutneys, infused oils
- Use on a menu
- Benefits

Resource: Books

Simple Cuisine: The Easy New Approach to Four-Star Cooking. Jean-Georges Vongerichten. Prentice Hall. New York, 1990.

The Sauce Bible: A Guide to the Saucier's Craft. David Paul Larousse. John Wiley & Sons, Inc. New York, 1993.
Sauces: Classical and Contemporary Sauce Making. James Peterson. Van Nostrand Reinhold. New York, 1991.

TOPIC: Ways to vary or replace classic sauces for a more healthful meal
- Lighter versions of cream sauces
- Replacing meat base with vegetables
- Substitutes for hollandaise, bearnaise, and beurre blancs

Resource: Magazine

Eating Well, including "Rx for Recipes," bimonthly feature
Cooking Light

Resources: Book

Techniques of Healthy Cooking. Culinary Institute of America. Mary Donovan, ed. Van Nostrand Reinhold. New York, 1993

TOPIC: What is the purpose of a sauce?

Assignments

1 While preparing a beurre blanc, the sauté chef notices that the sauce has become thick and it is difficult to add more butter. Why is this?
   - If cream has been used, the cream has reduced too much, so the sauce is too thick.
   - Enough butter has been added.
   - Temperature under pan is too low.
   - See also pages 317, 335–337.
2 The hollandaise has a curdled appearance. What is the problem? Can this be repaired?
   - The sauce is "broken." The eggs may have been too cold. They should be about the same temperature as the butter. Stop adding butter and continue to whip over the simmering water until it loses its curdled appearance. Then resume adding butter.

- If the water under the sauce boils, or the butter is too hot, the eggs may "scramble." Add cold water to the sauce and whip until the sauce is smooth. It may be necessary to strain the sauce. In that case you may need to add more eggs.
- See also pages 332–335.

3 The barbecue sauce has a greasy sheen. What can be done?
- The sauce should be degreased by skimming before serving.
- If time allows, cool sauce and refrigerate to allow grease to solidify on surface.
- See also page 339.

4 The liquid from the salsa runs all over the plate. How can it be fixed?
- The salsa can be strained prior to plating.
- Serve salsa in a ramekin or small dish instead of spooning onto plate.

5 "Hunger is the best sauce." (Young's Cicero) What exactly does this mean?

6 Explain any problems/difficulties with the following menu items (actual menu items from existing restaurants):
Sautéed softshell crab crusted in coconut and pecans with red chili linguini in a cilantro-pineapple sauce.
Hickory-roasted breast of chicken with Scotch-bonnet herb marinade, cilantro rice with mango-banana salsa.
- The plate presentations appear to be too busy.
- There are too many flavors that may not blend.
- The customer may not be able to envision the dish when reading the menu description.
- Leave out some of the adjectives.
- Leave out some of the ingredients.

Answer Key to Self-Study Questions

1 It allows the starches in the flour to expand quickly, beginning the process of thickening almost immediately.

2 Light velouté—10–12 ounces roux to 1 gallon stock; used for soups
Medium velouté—12–16 ounces roux to 1 gallon stock; used for sauces
Heavy velouté—18–20 ounces roux to 1 gallon stock; used for a binder

3 (a) Impurities, if not removed, could compromise the color, texture, and flavor of the finished sauce.
   (b) Pulling the pot slightly off the center of the burner allows the natural convection of the simmering liquid to throw the impurities to one side of the pot.

4
- Full, rich, well-balanced flavor, predominantly of roasted veal
- Deep brown color that is also translucent and glossy
- Perfect nappé in body and texture

5
- The wringing method—twisting the ends of sauce-filled cheesecloth in opposite directions over a bowl
- The milking method—holding two corners of a piece of cheesecloth over a bowl and lifting alternating corners until all the sauce is strained through.

6
- Finishing with a fortified wine
- Reduction
- Finishing with butter

7 To coat with sauce; thickened to a point at which a liquid will evenly coat the back of a spoon.

8 It is easy to miss the early signs of souring or the presence of odors absorbed from the reach-in or walk-in when the milk is very cold. A small amount should be brought to a boil and then checked for a sweet smell and smooth appearance, with no evidence of curdling or off aromas.

9
- Plum tomatoes
- Tomato purée
- Ground salt pork, oil, or clarified butter
- Stock
- Diced aromatic vegetables
- Sachet d'epices or bouquet garni
- Any additional flavoring or seasoning items

10 Contemporary Sauces:
- Generally take less time to prepare than grand sauces.
- Are more likely to be tailored to a specific dish.
- Have lighter color, texture, and flavor than grand sauces.
- Are more likely to be finished and/or thickened with emulsions, modified starches, or by reduction.
- Are less likely to contain roux.

Grand Sauces:
- Can be prepared in large batches, then flavored to produce "small sauces."

11
- Hollandaise—formed when melted or partially clarified butter is suspended in partially cooked egg yolks
- Beurre blanc—butter forms an emulsion with a reduction, occasionally stabilized with heavy cream
- Sauce vin blanc—depending on the method of preparation, one or both of above-described emulsions occurs

An emulsion is formed when two items that normally do not combine form a homogenous mixture; may be semipermanent or permanent.

12 (a) Cooking down an acid and flavoring ingredients (such as shallots and peppercorns) to a nearly dry or syrupy consistency.
(b) Gives the sauce a certain brightness of flavor and helps to moderate its richness.

13 Maximum of three hours.

14
- Velouté—its flavor should reflect the type of stock used in its preparation; pale ivory color with no hint of gray; translucent and lustrous with a sheen; perfectly smooth, noticeable body, thick enough to coat the back of a spoon, but still pourable from a ladle.
- Tomato—deep rich tomato flavor with no traces of bitterness, excess acidity, or sweetness; opaque in color but with some sheen; relatively smooth in texture though coarser than the other grand sauces, and thick enough to coat the back of a spoon, but thin enough to pour easily.
- Jus lié—as compared to demi-glace, a greater degree of translucence, clarity, and sheen, but with less complex flavor and lighter in texture and color.
- Béchamel—creamy flavor with no taste of roux; slightly ivory in color; opaque but with a definite sheen, and perfectly smooth with no graininess.
- Hollandaise—lemon color with a satin smooth texture and appearance, the aroma of good butter, and a light, almost frothy consistency.
- Beurre blanc—similar to a hollandaise, but lighter in color and body; pale yellow and creamy without oiliness.

15 Whole butter combined with herbs or other seasonings and usually used to "sauce" grilled or broiled items or vegetables.

Keywords

Béchamel: A white sauce made of milk thickened with light roux and flavored with onion. It is one of the GRAND SAUCES.

Beurre blanc (Fr.): "White butter." A classic emulsified sauce made with a reduction of white wine and shallots thickened with whole butter and possibly finished with fresh herbs or other seasonings.

Brown sauce: One of the classic grand sauces made by thickening a very rich brown veal stock with a roux. Used as is or to prepare demi-glace, or "small" or derivative sauces.

Compound butter: Whole butter combined with herbs or other seasonings and usually used to sauce grilled or broiled items or vegetables.

Confit: Meat (usually goose, duck, or pork) cooked and preserved in its own fat.

Coulis: A thick purée, usually of vegetables but possibly of fruit. (Traditionally meat, fish, or shellfish purée; meat jus; or certain thick soups.)

Cuisson (Fr.): Poaching liquid, including stock, fumet, court bouillon, or other liquid, which may be reduced and used as a base for the poached item's sauce.

Demi-glace (Fr.): "Half-glaze." A mixture of equal proportions of brown stock and brown sauce that has been reduced by half. One of the GRAND SAUCES.

Derivatives: Sauces prepared by modifying a base sauce (demi-glace, béchamel, or velouté, for instance).

Emulsion sauce: Sauce made by suspending two substances which normally will not mix into a permanent or temporary mixture. Hot emulsion sauces include hollandaise and beurre blanc; cold sauces include mayonnaise and vinaigrette.

Espagnole sauce (Fr.): "Spanish sauce." Brown sauce made with brown stock, caramelized mirepoix and tomato purée, and seasonings.

Fond (Fr.): Stock.

Grand sauce: One of several basic sauces that are used in the preparation of many other small sauces. The grand sauces are: demi-glace, velouté, béchamel, hollandaise, and tomato. (Also called Mother Sauce.)

Hollandaise: A classic emulsion sauce made with a vinegar reduction, egg yolks, and melted butter flavored with lemon juice. It is one of the GRAND SAUCES.

Jus lié (Fr.): Meat juice thickened lightly with arrowroot or cornstarch.

Modified starch: A starch that has been purified; used to thicken products. Examples include cornstarch and arrowroot.

Monté au beurre (Fr.): "To lift with butter." A technique used to enrich sauces, thicken them slightly, and give them a glossy appearance by whisking in whole butter.

Napper/Nappé (Fr.): To coat with sauce; thickened.

Sauce vin blanc (Fr.): Literally "white wine sauce." Made by combining a reduced cooking liquid with prepared hollandaise, velouté, or diced butter.

Sweat/sweating: To cook an item, usually vegetables, in a covered pan in a small amount of fat until it softens and releases moisture.

Tomato sauce: A sauce prepared by simmering tomatoes in a liquid (water or broth) with aromatics. One of the GRAND SAUCES.

Velouté: A sauce of white stock (chicken, veal, seafood) thickened with white roux; one of the GRAND SAUCES.

Dry-Heat Cooking Methods

Objectives

- Explain the following dry-heat techniques:
    Grilling, broiling, barbecuing (pages 344–349)
    Roasting and baking (pages 349–354)
    Poêléing (pages 357–358)
    Sautéing, and two variations (pages 358–364)
    Pan-frying (pages 364–367)
    Deep-frying (pages 367–371)
- Understand what cuts of meat, poultry, and fish are best suited for which dry-heat cooking techniques (interspersed throughout chapter)
- Describe how to make gravies and jus liés for roasted items (page 354)
- Describe how to make sauces for sautéed foods (page 362)
- Explain standard breading procedure (page 366)
- Understand how to select and maintain frying oil (page 368)

Lecture Outline

THE DRY-HEAT COOKING METHODS
  Grilling, Broiling and Barbecuing
    Mise en Place
      1. Assemble all ingredients and preparations used for grilling.
        - Meats, fish, poultry, breads, vegetables, fruits
        - Oils for lubricating both the food and the grill's rods
        - Seasonings and flavorings
        - Additional and optional items, as desired
      2. Assemble and prepare all equipment necessary for grilling.
    Method
      1. Place the food on the grill to start cooking and "mark" it.
      2. Turn once to cook on second side.
      3. Finish to desired doneness and serve at once.
  Roasting and Baking
    Mise en Place
      1. Assemble all ingredients and preparations for roasting.
        - Main item: meat, fish, poultry, vegetable, or fruit

- Barding, larding, or other flavoring/ moisturizing ingredients
- Stuffings, coatings, crusts, and seasoning mixtures
- Stock or brown sauce and other items required (bones, mirepoix, tomato product, and deglazing liquid)

2. Assemble all equipment necessary for preparation and service.

Method

1. Sear the food as appropriate and baste throughout cooking time.
2. Cook foods to the correct doneness, and allow them to rest briefly.
3. Prepare the pan gravy or jus, if desired.
4. Carve (optional) and serve with appropriate sauce and/or garnish.

Sidebar *Keeping Roasts Lean and Moist*
Carryover Cooking
Preparing Jus or Pan Gravy for Roasted Foods
Carving
Standing Rib Roast

1. Lay the rib roast on its side.
2. Use the knife tip to cut the slice of meat away from the bone and serve it.

Leg of Lamb

1. To steady the leg, hold the shank bone firmly in one hand with a clean side towel. Make parallel cuts from the shank end down to the bone.
2. Continue cutting slices of meat from the leg, cutting away from the bone to make even slices.
3. When the slices become very large, begin to cut the meat at a slight angle, first from the left side, then from the right side, alternating until the leg is entirely sliced.

Birds

1. Use a knife tip to cut through the skin at the point where the leg meets the breast. Use the tines of a kitchen fork to gently press the leg away from the body. A properly roasted bird's leg will come away easily.
2. Use one kitchen fork to hold the breast

steady. Insert another kitchen fork at the joint between the drumstick and the thigh. Pull the leg away from the body. Repeat for the other leg.

3. Cut the leg into two pieces through the joint between the thigh and the drumstick.
4. Cut through the skin on the breast on either side of the breastbone to begin to remove the breast meat.
5. Use the tines of a kitchen fork to gently pull the breast meat away from the rib cage. Make short, smooth strokes with the knife tip to cut the meat cleanly and completely away.

Poêléing
Mise en Place

1. Assemble all ingredients and preparations for poêléing.
   - Main item: lean white meats
   - Matignon
   - Butter (melted)
   - Stock or a prepared jus for sauce
   - Thickener if necessary
2. Assemble all equipment necessary for preparation and service.

Method

1. Sear or seize the main item.
2. Sweat or smother the matignon in batter.
3. Baste with additional butter (optional), cover, and cook in oven until properly cooked.
4. Prepare the sauce as you would a pan gravy. Carve the item if necessary, and serve.

Sautéing
Mise en Place

1. Assemble all ingredients and preparations used for sautéing.
   - Main item: boneless meat, poultry, eggs, fish, vegetable, or fruit
   - Marinades, stuffings, or special seasonings
   - Flour for dredging
   - Cooking fat or oil

- Base sauce or stock
- Additional ingredients for finishing or garnishing the sauce

2. Assemble all equipment necessary for preparation and service.

Method

1. Place food into preheated oil and let it cook until browned or golden.
2. Turn the item(s) once.
3. Remove the food from the pan while preparing the sauce (if any), add the appropriate flavoring or garnishing ingredients and serve at once on heated plates.

Making Sauces for Sautéed Foods

1. Remove any excess fat or oil.
2. Add aromatic ingredients or garnish items that need to be cooked, such as garlic, shallots, mushrooms, and ginger.
3. Deglaze the pan, releasing the reduced drippings from the pan.
4. Add the base sauce and any other ingredients intended to add flavor, texture, and color.
5. Add garnish and finishing ingredients.

Variation on Sautéing Method
Scrambling Eggs and Preparing Omelets
Stir-Frying

Pan-Frying

Mise en Place

1. Assemble all ingredients and preparations for pan-frying.
   - Main item: meat, poultry, fish, vegetable
   - Breadings, batters, or other coatings
   - Oil
   - Stuffings, marinades, or seasoning mixtures
   - Ingredients for sauce and gravy
2. Assemble all equipment necessary for preparation and service.

Method

1. Heat oil to correct temperature for food being cooked.
2. Add food to hot oil and keep oil and/or food in motion.

3. Brown on first side, then turn the food once.
4. Finish in pan or uncovered in oven.
5. Sauce and serve while hot.

Sidebar *Standard Breading Procedure*
Deep-Frying
Sidebar *Fat and Oil Selection and Maintenance*

Mise en Place

1. Assemble all ingredients and preparations for deep-frying.
   - Main item being prepared: meat, poultry, fish, vegetable
   - Batters, breading, coatings (optional)
   - Oil
   - Separately prepared sauce
2. Assemble all equipment necessary for preparation and service.
   - Frying kettle or fryolator
   - Basket, spider, skimmer
   - Tongs
   - Set up to blot/drain after frying
   - Container to finish in oven or hold warm
   - Serving pieces

Method

1. Place prepared item directly into oil.
   Swimming Method
   Basket Method
   Double-basket Method
2. Cook foods to the proper color and doneness.
3. Drain or blot and serve while very hot.

SUMMARY

Discussion Topics

TOPIC: Benefits of dry-heat cooking with and without fats and oils.

TOPIC: New techniques/unusual techniques
- Stone cooking
- Fondue
- Grilling
- Smoking

TOPIC: Why smoke?
• Aroma
• Flavor
• Texture—curing process
• Color
• Preservation

TOPIC: Types of wood to smoke with:
• New England—East coast
   Hickory
   Oak
• Texas—Southwest
   Mesquite: it is a soft wood but burned first
   and used like charcoal or wet, with water.
• New Mexico
   Pecan wood

TOPIC: What foods can be smoked?
• Fish, meat
• Sausages
• Cheese (hard)
• Nuts, vegetables

TOPIC: Vegetables
• Roasting/grilling/smoking
   improve flavors, especially important for vegetarian dishes
   creates new flavors for entrées and sides
• Sauté
• Fry (batter-dipped, flour-dusted)

TOPIC: Egg cookery
• Scrambled
• Omelet
• Fried
• Baked/shirred

TOPIC: Plating and Presentation
• Classic
• Contemporary

Resource: Magazines

Food Arts
Chef

Bon Appetit
Food and Wine

Additional material for this chapter may be found
in the back of this manual. See the charts on broilers and grills, marking steaks, broiling meat and
fish, roasting, sautéing, pan-frying, deep-frying,
and enemies of fat.

Assignments

1   Saturday night at the Bedrock Grill, it seems
   that everything that could go wrong has. In the
   following situations (A-H), give some possible
   reasons for the problems and suggest some solutions:
   A. The pan-smoked chicken had an acrid, un-
      appetizing taste.
      • Pan-smoking should be done for a very
         short time. If an item is pan-smoked too
         long, it will produce an unappetizing
         product—too smokey.
      • Select hardwood chips with less-
         pronounced flavor.
      • If smoking is desired in conjunction with
         slow cooking, a smoker is recommended.
      • See also pages 350, 419.
   B. The roast looks good, but when it is sliced,
      the meat is dry, rubbery, and tough. The jus
      lié prepared from the drippings has a
      harsh, bitter flavor.
      • The roast may be overcooked. Take the
         temperature, so meat does not overcook
         or burn.
      • Remember to allow for carryover cooking
         when determining correct internal tem-
         perature for pulling the roast from the
         oven.
      • Mirepoix and trimmings may be over-
         cooked.
      • Drippings may be burnt.
      • Make a separate sauce or jus if drippings
         and/or mirepoix are scorched.
      • See also pages 349–355.

C. The chef grilled a halved duck. The duck was moist in some parts and dry in others.
- The fat in the dark meat will keep it from drying out as quickly.
- The breast will cook faster and get dry.
- Separate the pieces and cook them separately.
- Marinate the duck first.
- See also pages 344–349.

D. A platter of fried chicken is returned to the kitchen. Upon examination, it appears pale in color and soggy, and some of the pieces are not properly cooked through.
- The chicken was probably not cooked long enough.
- Oil may have been at too-low a temperature.
- Batter or breading may be too thick.
- May have been cooked in advance and held too long.
- See also pages 367–371.

E. One of the evening's specials is a chicken croquette. Several customers have ordered it, but the first three orders have been returned to the kitchen because they taste like fish, are nearly black in color, and the coating has a bitter taste. The chef noticed when the first orders were fired that there was a great deal of foam and smoking. The special is deleted from the menu immediately, of course, and the guests who received the unacceptable croquettes are compensated.
- Whenever possible, a separate fryolater should be used to fry fish items.
- The oil was much too hot, this is evident by the amount of smoke and foam.
- The oil is breaking down, which might be caused by:
    - excessive heat for too long of a period of time
    - salt
    - moisture
    - food particles
    - exposure to air

- The oil should be filtered or changed between shifts or daily.
- The chef was correct to delete the special. This should have been caught when the first order was cooked (they were almost black), not after three orders were returned.
- The chef should have prepared a test batch first and these problems would have been noticed by the chef rather than unhappy customers.
- See also page 368.

F. One of the assistants to the sauté chef was asked to slice the tenderloin of beef into 6-ounce portions. The first order that is prepared that evening seems to be shrinking too much as it cooks, and it doesn't look exactly right. When it is cut open (the sauté chef is not willing to send it out that way), it is very tough.
- Most likely, the assistant misidentified the cut of beef.
- More training and supervision might be necessary.
- See also pages 263, 266.

G. The French fries are coming out very dark, but not properly cooked.
- The French fries may have been cooked only once. It is best to par-cook (blanch) French fries prior to service. At service time, they can be cooked quickly at a high heat and the finished product will be crisp and cooked thoroughly.
- The oil might be too hot.
- See also Question 1, E, above.
- See also pages 367–371.

H. The baked potatoes at the beginning of service are delicious, fresh, and earthy tasting, but by the end of the night the skins are soft and flabby and the flesh has a slightly sweet taste.
- This might be the result if the potatoes were cooked and held in foil. The foil will cause the potatoes to steam rather than bake.

- The potatoes may have been baked properly but held too long in a warming drawer.
- The potatoes might be better if they are baked in batches through the course of the evening rather than all at once.
- The potatoes may have been improperly stored (e.g., in refrigerator) before cooking.
- See also pages 233–234.

2 Fried foods are often very popular, but some customers may hesitate to order them because they are high in calories and fats. Describe the characteristic flavors, textures, aromas, and colors you associate with fried foods. How could you achieve those characteristics by using an alternative technique or approach?

   Fried foods, e.g.:
- Brown exterior
- Crisp exterior/crunchy
- Juicy
- Filling
   Alternatives, e.g.:
- Searing in dry skillet or on broiler/grill for crisp exterior
- Baking with crisp coating
- Cooking at high temperatures very quickly on grill or in oven

3 Everyone has at least a certain degree of "prejudice" about vegetables. What are some ways to overcome personal preferences about long-time vegetable likes and dislikes?
- Try roasting, grilling, or smoking the vegetables for a new flavor.
- Experiment with "ethnic" seasonings.
- Incorporate vegetables into well-liked dishes and comfort foods, such as, carrots in chili, puréed parsnips in mashed potatoes, grilled vegetables in sandwiches, and "classics" like peas in macaroni and cheese.

4 Sautéing is a cooking technique often perceived as requiring the greatest skills or abilities. Why do you think this is true?
- Ability to gauge doneness.

- Ability to match food to technique.
- Foods prepared by sautéing are often expensive, therefore novice cooks would not be trusted to handle.
- Required ability to select and prepare appropriate sauces.
- See also pages 358–362.

5 Grilling, barbecuing, and broiling techniques are almost as popular as sautéing (more so, in some restaurants). Why?
- Associated with "trendy" cuisines such as Tex Mex (and other regional American cuisines), Mediterranean, Caribbean.
- Quick method with some "new" popular feature items: vegetables, pizza/breads, fruits, fish.
- Healthy alternative to cooking in fats.
- Barbecuing and some related techniques (e.g., smoking and blackening) are more difficult to do at home.
- See also pages 344–349.

6 When potatoes were first introduced to Europe, they were not an immediate success. In fact, they were considered poisonous, and were at first grown strictly for their foliage. Today, most cuisines have dishes that feature potatoes. Name some of the potato dishes that come to mind when a particular cuisine is mentioned. (French, German, English, etc.). Consider both dry- and-moist heat cooking techniques.
- French
   French fries—dry with fat
   Savoyarde—moist
   Dauphinoise—moist
   Châteaubriand Potatoes—dry with fat
   Potatoes Anna—dry with fat
   Duchesse—moist
   Lorette—moist
   Croquette/Berny—dry with fat
   Souffled Potatoes—dry with fat
- German
   German Potato Salad—moist
- Swiss
   Roësti Potatoes—dry with fat

- English
  Chips (fish and chips)—dry with fat
- Italian
  Potato Gnocchi—moist
- See also pages 170, 172, 233–234.

7 The scrambled eggs on the breakfast bar at the hotel dining room are unappealing, watery, and a bright brassy color.
- Scrambled eggs do not hold well. They should be prepared in small batches and brought to the chafing dish as needed.
- An alternative would be to offer made-to-order omelets. This would increase labor costs but might attract new clientele.
- Another alternative would be to offer other egg dishes, such as poached, shirred eggs or quiche—with or without crust—that will hold longer on a buffet line.
- See also page 362.

Answer Key to Self-Study Questions

1 (a) Areas that are hotter versus areas that are cooler may also refer to areas on the grill designated to avoid flavor transfers.
  (b) Cook at the best temperatures to preserve the optimum flavors.
2 • Proper cross-hatch marking
  • Slightly charred flavor
  • A moist interior
3 Simulates broiling by cooking an item in a hot pan with little or no fat.
4 To introduce additional flavor and moisture.
5 Item is placed on a large skewer or spit over, or in front of, an open flame or other radiant heat source; constant turning: drip pan used to collect drippings.
6 • Baked: May be portion size or smaller; vegetables or fruits; items made in bakeshop.
  • Roasted: Larger cuts of meat, whole birds. Distinction is more a matter of terminology and usage than of method.
7 (a) Heat is retained in cooked food, allowing it to continue cooking even after removal

from the cooking medium if not removed soon enough.
  (b) Foods can overcook after being removed from the oven.
8 (a) Select proper cuts, shapes, and sizes.
  (b) Be able to gauge the exact point at which food is perfectly cooked to customer preference.
9 (a) Sautéing: Light dusting with flour only (optional); cooked in little oil; cooked over high heat; product's natural juices are released into pan; sauce may be made in same pan
  (b) Pan-frying: Usually battered or breaded; cooked in larger quantity of oil; cooked over less-intense heat; natural juices sealed in (not released in pan); any sauce must be made in a separate pan
10 Food was allowed to overcook, food was cooked too far in advance, food was cooked at a temperature higher than required, or an inappropriate cut of meat was used.
11 Arrowroot or cornstarch is used to make a jus lié; flour or roux is used for a pan gravy.
12 White meats and small game
  (1) Sear or "seize" the item
  (2) Sweat matignon
  (3) Baste with additional butter, cover and place in a hot oven
  (4) Remove casserole and prepare a sauce
  (5) Add thickener to finish the sauce
  (6) Carve and serve
13 Scrambling eggs, preparing omelets, and stir-frying.
14 (1) Limp and translucent
  (2) Crisp and deep brown
  (3) Rich mahogany with a melting texture
15 If items are crowded the temperature will drop and a good crust will not form; if the pan is too large, the drippings can scorch. Too much oil can result in a greasy finished product; not enough oil can result in scorching, tearing, or burning.
16 (1) Dry the main item; dip it in flour; shake off any excess.

(2) Transfer the item to egg wash.

(3) Transfer the item to a container of bread crumbs.

(4) Pack the bread crumbs around the item evenly; transfer to a holding tray.

17 • Store in a cool, dry area, away from strong lights.

• Use high-quality oil to begin with.

• Prevent contact from copper, brass, or bronze metals which hasten breakdown.

• Thoroughly dry items to be fried before placing them in the oil.

• Avoid salting products over the fryer.

• Don't overheat the oil.

• Turn the fryer off after use and keep oil covered between uses.

• Constantly remove any small particles of food that come off in the oil.

• Filter the oil after each shift, or daily.

• Discard the oil if it becomes rancid, smokes below 350°F (176°C), foams excessively, or turns dark brown.

18 • Oil was not hot enough

• The fryer was crowded

• The oil was old and/or improperly handled

• The oil was used to fry strongly flavored foods

• The food was held too long

• The breading or batter was applied too heavily

Keywords

A l'anglaise (Fr.): (1) Foods that have been breaded and fried; (2) foods that have been boiled.

A la meunière (Fr.): Dishes prepared in the style of the miller's wife (dusted with flour, sautéed, served with hot butter, lemon, and parsley).

Baking: A cooking method used to describe foods prepared in an oven; similar to roasting.

Barbecue; barbecuing: A cooking method involving grilling food over a wood or charcoal fire. Usually some sort of marinade or sauce is brushed on the item during cooking.

Bard; barding: To cover an item with slabs or strips of fat, such as bacon or fatback, to baste it during roasting. The fat is usually tied on with butcher's twine.

Broil; broiling: A cooking method in which items are cooked by a radiant heat source placed above the food.

Carryover cooking: Heat retained in cooked foods that allows them to continue cooking even after removal from the cooking medium. Especially important to roasted foods.

Deep-fry; deep-frying: A cooking method in which foods are cooked by immersion in hot fat; deep-fried foods are often coated with bread crumbs or batter before being cooked.

Grill; grilling: A cooking technique in which foods are cooked by a radiant heat source placed below the food. Also, the piece of equipment on which grilling is done. Grills may be fueled by gas, electricity, charcoal, or wood.

Jus (Fr.): Juice. Jus de viande is meat gravy. Meat served au jus is served with its own juice or jus lié.

Jus lié (Fr.): Meat juice thickened lightly with arrowroot or cornstarch.

Larding: Inserting strips of fatback (or, in some cases spices or garlic) into a cut of meat, fish, or poultry to improve final texture (moisture) and/or flavor.

Mark: To turn foods during grilling so that they are seared with a pattern of the grill rods.

Matignon (Fr.): An edible mirepoix that is often used in poêléed dishes and is usually served with the finished dish. Typically, matignon includes two parts carrot, one part celery, one part leek, one part onion, one part mushroom (optional), and one part ham or bacon.

Omelet: Beaten egg that is cooked in butter in a specialized pan or skillet and then rolled or folded into an oval. Omelets may be filled with a variety of ingredients before or after rolling.

Pan-broiling: A cooking method similar to dry sautéing that simulates broiling by cooking an item in a hot pan with little or no fat.

Pan-frying: A cooking method in which items are cooked in deep fat in a skillet; this generally involves more fat than sautéing or stir-frying but less than deep-frying.

Pan gravy: A sauce made by deglazing pan drippings from a roast and combining them with a roux or other starch and additional stock.

Poêlé/poêléing: A method in which items are cooked in their own juices (usually with the addition of a matignon, other aromatics, and melted butter) in a covered pot, usually in the oven. (Also called butter roasting).

Resting period: Time allowed for roasted or baked items to even out internal temperature; time elapsed between removal from the oven and time of carving and/or serving food.

Roast/roasting: A cooking method in which items are cooked in an oven or on a spit over a fire.

Sauté, sautéing: A cooking method in which items are cooked quickly in a small amount of fat in a pan on the range top.

Scrambled eggs: Eggs prepared by blending yolks and white until homogenous, then cooking in a sauté pan over direct heat while stirring constantly to form soft masses, or curds.

Sear: To brown the surface of food in fat over high heat before finishing by another method (for example, braising) in order to add flavor.

Seize: To stiffen the exterior of foods without browning them.

Smoke-roasting: A method for roasting foods in which items are placed on a rack in a pan containing wood chips that smolder, emitting smoke, when the pan is placed on the range top or in the oven.

Spit-roasting: To roast an item on a large skewer or spit over, or in front of, an open flame or other radiant heat source.

Standard breading procedure: The assembly-line procedure in which items are dredged in flour, dipped in beaten egg, then coated with bread crumbs before being pan-fried or deep-fried.

Stir-fry/stir-frying: A cooking method similar to sautéing in which items are cooked over very high heat, using little fat. Usually this is done in a wok and the food is kept moving constantly.

Zones: Specific areas that have desirable characteristics, such as hotter and cooler areas on a grill, cooler and coldest areas in a walk-in. Established to make work and food storage procedures more efficient.

CHAPTER   1 0

Moist-Heat and Combination Cooking Techniques

Objectives

- Name the mise en place and methods for the following moist-heat techniques:
    Steaming (pages 374–380)
    Poaching (pages 380–386)
    Stewing (pages 394–397)
    Braising (pages 391–394)
    Simmering (pages 386–388)
    Boiling (pages 388–391)
- Identify the kinds and cuts of food best suited to each of these techniques (interspersed throughout)
- Determine the proper doneness of items cooked with moist-heat and combination techniques (page 378)
- Name some variations on moist-heat techniques used to prepare eggs, various grains, legumes, vegetables, and fruits (pages 388–391)

Lecture Outline

STEAMING AND ITS VARIATIONS
- Steaming
- Preparing foods *en papillote*
- Shallow-poaching
- Pan-steaming
Steaming
  Mise en Place
    1. Assemble all ingredients and preparations for steaming.
        - Main ingredient(s)
- Steaming liquid
- Additional or optional items for flavoring, finishing, and garnishing
- Sauce or items necessary to prepare sauce
    2. Assemble all equipment necessary for cooking and serving.
        - Steamer, steamer insert, or other equipment for steaming
        - Steamer racks, pans, or inserts
        - Tongs, spoons, spatulas
        - Serving pieces

Method
1. Bring the liquid to a full boil in a covered vessel.
2. Add the main item to the steamer on a rack in a single layer.
3. Replace the lid and allow the steam to build up again.
4. Steam the main item to the correct doneness.
5. Serve the food immediately on heated plates with an appropriate sauce.

Sidebar *Determining Doneness for Moist-Heat Methods*

Cooking Foods en Papillote
Mise en Place
1. Assemble all ingredients and preparations for *en papillote.*
   - Main item(s)
   - Broth or sauce
   - Additional or optional flavoring, seasoning, or garnishing items
2. Assemble all equipment necessary for cooking and serving.
   - Parchment paper
   - Sizzler platters or baking sheets
   - Serving pieces
Method
1. Assemble the packages.
2. Place the bag on a preheated sizzler platter and put it in a very hot oven.

Shallow-Poaching
Mise en Place
1. Assemble all ingredients and preparations for shallow-poaching.
   - Main ingredient(s)
   - Liquid
   - Additional or optional items for flavoring, finishing, and garnishing
   - Items necessary to prepare the sauce
2. Assemble all equipment necessary for cooking and serving.
   - Sauté pan, or other suitable cooking vessel
   - Parchment or loose-fitting lid
   - Serving pieces as needed: strainers, whip, tongs, etc.

Method
1. Add the ingredients to the pan.
2. Add the main item and the cooking liquid.
3. Bring the liquid to a bare simmer over direct heat.
4. Lightly cover the sauté pan with parchment paper and finish cooking the main item either over direct heat or in a moderate oven.
5. Transfer the main item to a holding dish. Moisten it with a small amount of the cooking liquid. Cover and keep warm.
6. Prepare a sauce from the cooking liquid.
7. Ladle the sauce over the food and serve it while still very hot.

Making a Sauce from the Cooking Liquid
Pan-Steaming
Mise en Place
1. Assemble all ingredients and preparations for pan-steaming.
2. Assemble all equipment necessary for cooking and serving.
Method
1. Bring the liquid to a boil in a pan.
2. Add the food being pan-steamed in a single layer.
3. Cover the pan and cook until the food is properly done.

The Submersion Techniques: Poaching and Simmering
Ingredient Selection for the Submersion Techniques
Poaching
Mise en Place
1. Assemble all ingredients and preparations for poaching.
   - Main ingredient(s)
   - Liquid
   - Additional or optional items for flavoring, finishing, and garnishing
   - Items necessary to prepare sauce
2. Assemble all equipment necessary for cooking and serving.
   - Poacher or other appropriately sized pot

- Ladles or skimmers
- Holding containers to keep foods warm (optional)
- Carving boards and slicers (optional)
- Instant-reading thermometer

Method

1. Combine the food to be poached with the liquid and bring to the correct cooking temperature.
2. Maintain the proper cooking speed throughout the poaching process.
3. Carefully remove the main item to a holding container and moisten it with some of the liquid to prevent it from drying out while the sauce is being prepared.
4. Serve the food at the appropriate temperature with the necessary sauces and garnish.

Simmering and Boiling

Mise en Place

1. Assemble all ingredients and preparations for simmering and boiling.
   - Main ingredient(s)
   - Liquid
   - Additional or optional items for flavoring, finishing, and garnishing
   - Items necessary to prepare sauce
2. Assemble all equipment necessary for cooking and serving.
   - Poacher or other pot
   - Ladles or skimmers
   - Strainers or colanders
   - Holding containers to keep foods warm or to hold once cooled (optional)
   - Carving boards and slicers (optional)
   - Instant-reading thermometer

Method

1. Combine the food to be simmered or boiled with the liquid and bring to the correct cooking temperature.
2. Maintain the proper cooking speed throughout the simmering or boiling process.
3. Carefully remove the main item as appropriate.

Special Boiling Methods
  Pasta
  Spaetzle
  Pilaf
  Polenta and Other Cereals
  Risotto

THE COMBINATION COOKING METHODS

Braising

Mise en Place

1. Assemble all ingredients for braising.
   - Main item(s)
   - Cooking fat or oil (optional in some cases)
   - Braising liquid
   - Additional or optional flavoring, seasoning, or garnishing items
   - Thickener for sauce (optional in some cases)
2. Assemble all equipment necessary for cooking and serving.
   - Deep pot with lid (or other cooking vessel)
   - Kitchen fork to test doneness
   - Carving knife, if necessary
   - Equipment as needed to finish sauce

Method

1. Sear the main item in hot oil or blanch in a liquid.
2. Remove the main item and add the mirepoix.
3. Add the appropriate amount of liquid.
4. Return the main item, cover the pot, and place it in a moderate oven.
5. Add the sachet d'epices or bouquet garni and vegetable garnish at the appropriate times, to ensure proper flavor extraction and cooking.
6. Remove the lid during the final portion of the cooking time.
7. Remove the main item from the braising liquid when it is properly cooked.
8. Place the pot over direct heat and continue to reduce the sauce to develop its flavor, body, and consistency.
9. Strain the sauce.

10. Carve or slice the main item and serve it on heated plates with the sauce and an appropriate garnish.

Sidebar *Glossary of Braises and Stews*

Stewing

Mise en Place

1. Assemble all ingredients and preparations for stewing.
   - Main item(s)
   - Cooking fat or oil (optional in some cases)
   - Cooking liquid
   - Additional or optional flavoring, seasoning, or garnishing items
   - Thickener for sauce (optional in some cases)
2. Assemble all equipment necessary for cooking and serving.
   - Deep pot with lid (or other cooking vessel)
   - Kitchen fork to test doneness
   - Equipment as needed to finish sauce

Method

1. Sear the main item in hot oil or blanch it by placing it in a pot of cold stock or water and bringing the liquid to a boil.
2. Remove the main item from the pot and add the mirepoix.
3. Return the main item to the mirepoix bed in the pot; add the appropriate cooking liquid and bring it to a simmer.
4. Cover the pot and place it in a moderate oven, or cook it over direct heat on the stove top.
5. Add the aromatics and vegetable garnish, if necessary or desired, at the appropriate time to ensure proper cooking and extraction of flavor.
6. Stew the food until a piece of the main item is tender to the bite.
7. Finish the stew by adding any additional thickeners or liaison, garnish ingredients, or final seasoning adjustments.
8. Serve the stew on heated plates with the sauce and the appropriate garnish.

SUMMARY

Discussion Topics

TOPIC: Ethnic dishes that use steaming
- Dim sum (Chinese)
- Tamales (Latin)
- *En papillote* (French)
- Couscous (Middle Eastern)

TOPIC: Ways to improve flavor of poached or steamed foods:
- Cooking technique (do not overcook or undercook)
- Aromatics (in poaching or steaming liquid)
- Herb and spice blends (on product, after cooking)
- Tomato product (add to sauces, condiments, or other accompaniments)

TOPIC: Vegetables
- Steam
- Boil

TOPIC: Pasta, dumplings, and noodles
- Fresh vs. dried
- Variety by cuisine
- Filled and flat types
- Preparing fresh pasta
- Flavoring and coloring fresh pasta

TOPIC: Grains and beans that are growing in popularity
- Polenta
- Bulgar
- Frik
- Quinoa
- Kasha
- Adzuki beans
- Anasazi beans
- Fava beans

Additional material for this chapter may be found in the back of this manual. See the charts on boiling, simmering, shallow-poaching, and braising.

Assignments

1   The entremetier went home sick and an inexperienced prep cook has taken her place. Discuss what has happened in each situation below (A-H):

A. The long-grained rice was sticky and moist.
   • Too much water was added.
   • The rice was stirred too much.
   • The rice was overcooked.

B. The red cabbage has turned blue.
   • This is a natural occurance, especially in an alkaline environment. It can be avoided somewhat by adding an acid to the cooking medium—such as red wine, lemon juice, or vinegar.

C. The broccoli is brilliantly green and completely soft.
   • Baking soda was added to the cooking water to keep the color. This turns the vegetable to mush, destroys the vitamins, and ruins the flavor.

D. The potato purée is lumpy, heavy, and a little gray.
   • Undercooked
   • Not enough water
   • Oxidized before cooking (not held in enough water)

E. The risotto is not creamy.
   • A short-grain rice other than Arborio may have been used.
   • The risotto was not stirred sufficiently during cooking.
   • The right amount of stock and butter may not have been added.
   • The wine may have been added too early in the cooking process.

F. The beans are crunchy, even after they have simmered for an hour.
   • The beans may not have been soaked prior to cooking.
   • An acid or salt (used as a flavoring ingredient) may have been added too early in the cooking process.

G. The pasta sticks together and cannot be served.
   • The pasta may have been cooked in too little water, or it was not stirred sufficiently during cooking.
   • Not shocked and/or oiled after draining

H. The dumplings served with chicken stew are tough and heavy.
   • The dumpling batter may have been too thick.
   • The batter may have been overmixed.
   • The batter may have been mixed too far in advance.
   • See also pages 374–378, 386–391.

2   A Boiled New England Dinner is featured on the menu. But, on one particular evening, the vegetables appear gray and the meat is tough and stringy. What was wrong?
   • It was overcooked.
   • It was cooked in an aluminum pan.
   • See also pages 386–388.

3   The steamed snapper with a sake sauce seems bland, and the flesh of the snapper is almost dry. How could this be improved?
   • Add more seasoning to the sauce.
   • Serve with flavorful condiment, such as wasabi.
   Next time:
   • Pay careful attention to the cooking time.
   • Cook *en papillote.*
   • Wrap snapper in romaine or savoy cabbage leaves.
   • Consider another cooking technique.
   • See also pages 374–378.

4   The Yankee pot roast does not seem to have as full a flavor as usual, the meat is tough and hard to chew, and the sauce seems watery. What can be done to correct this?
   • The pot roast may not have been braised long enough. Return it with the sauce, cover and cook longer at low temperature. When the meat is tender enough, remove it from the sauce. Degrease the sauce, reduce, season and lié if it is still watery.
   • Remove the lid while the pot roast is nearly done cooking, so the liquid will begin to reduce and glaze will form on meat.
   • See also pages 391–395.

5 The hard-cooked eggs are hard to peel and have an unattractive green ring around the yolk. Why?
- The eggs were overcooked.
- The eggs were not cooled (shocked) immediately after cooking.
- The eggs were not peeled quickly after cooling.
- See also page 383–385.

6 The poached eggs are raggedy, and of the 50 that were poached, nearly half cannot be used because the yolk broke. What can be done to avoid this in the future?
- Add acid to the water (ratio: 1 tablespoon vinegar to each quart/liter).
- The eggs may be too fresh or too old—test one or two before cooking a large batch.

7 What are the special concerns related to cooking large quantities of vegetables, especially for banquets or institutional feeding situations (cafeterias, hospitals, airlines, prisons)?
- Commercial steamers are often used and overcooking is a problem
- Holding vegetables at correct temperatures/ without overcooking
- Seasoning appropriately for clientele—must be careful with salt and excessive "spicy" flavor
- Offering fresh vegetables (usually higher food and labor cost) whenever possible
- Frozen vegetables typically require shorter cooking time than fresh since they are blanched or parcooked during processing
- See also Steaming, pages 374–377.

8 The chef of a small bistro has heard that vegetarian and healthy entrées are becoming quite popular. He wants to drum up some new business, so he adds a few new menu items. However, the steamed vegetable plate is so boring even the vegetarians don't want to order it. The poached chicken Early Bird special isn't attracting the senior citizens. What could the chef do to improve his new menu selections?
- Be sure that poaching liquid for chicken is very flavorful.

- If the vegetables are steamed, they could be seasoned with aromatics and herbs.
- The vegetables and chicken could be roasted or grilled to give more flavor.
- Grains and beans could become the "center of the plate" or, particularly with the chicken, be included as sides on the plate.
- Hearty chutneys or spicy salsa could accompany either dish.
- Garnish the plates to improve eye appeal and offer a variety of textures on the plate.
- See also pages 17, 64–65.

9 Ethnic dishes based largely on grains and legumes have become popular on American menus in recent years. What do you think is the major reason for this new popularity?
- Grains and legumes are perceived as being "healthy."
- Mediterranean and Asian diets (and the FDA Food Guide Pyramid) all recommend many servings of grains and legumes as part of the daily diet.
- Usually the ethnic dishes incorporate spices and seasonings which are very appealing to our growing desire for "spicy" and flavorful food, making them more interesting than our basic rice pilaf or baked potato.
- See also pages 60, 67.

10 There are examples of dishes based on flours and meals, the principle components of virtually any cereal, pasta, noodle, or dumpling, pancake, and flatbreads in many cuisines. Discuss the ways in which these dishes are similar, and the ways in which each ethnic group has "individualized" these dishes. What are the similar uses of grains in different cultures?
- Most cultures have a type of pasta and/or dumpling—Cellophane noodles (Chinese), Soba and rice noodles (Japanese), semolina noodles (Italian), spaetzle (German), semolina gnocchi (Italian), egg noodles (American), stuffed dumplings (Chinese), bread dumplings (knaidel) (German), biscuit dumplings (American)—individualized by the sauces that they are served with: soy/

fish (Asian), brown sauce (German), tomato (Italian), cheese (American).

- Most cultures use flours and meals as a hot "cereal" mixed with milk, water, or stock (grits/polenta, semolina, farina). These cereals are also chilled to solidify, be cut, and reheated. Some are served sweet, some savory.
- Most cultures have a "pancake"—consider wonton skins (Chinese), rice paper (Japanese), crêpes (French), wheat and buckwheat pancakes (German, American), hoe cakes and Johnny cakes (American), and blinis (Eastern European). As with the cereals, some are served sweet and some savory.
- Most cultures have flatbreads—crostini, foccacia, ciabatta (all Italian), pita (Middle Eastern), poori, chapitas (both Indian), matzo (Eastern European) and corn and flour tortillas (Latin). All are individualized by the stuffings or toppings that accompany them.

11 Pasta, noodles, and various dumplings are often thought of as "comfort foods." What do you think this means, and why are these foods in particular, so often associated with home-style cooking?

- Comfort foods tend to be those foods that one grows up with, foods our mother made, foods from our homeland.
- Traditionally, foods such as pastas, noodles, and dumplings were often served in the home because they were filling and relatively inexpensive to prepare. Dried pastas are still convenient, inexpensive, and filling.
- As food preferences change, and people have less time to spend in the kitchen, they are less willing to make dumplings and noodles from "scratch." Now they can order these items in restaurants and still enjoy the satisfaction comfort food provides.
- What do you think will be the comfort food for the Class of 2010? Check out new food trends in magazines, *Food Arts, Restaurant Business, Restaurant News,* among others and newspapers, *Wall Street Journal,* and most city newspapers every Wednesday (traditionally food and restaurant day).

Answer Key to Self-Study Questions

1 Less-tender cuts of meat, stewing hens, some vegetables.
2 (1) Spread butter evenly in a cold pan; add aromatic ingredients and sweat.
   (2) Add the main item and the cooking liquid.
   (3) Bring to a bare simmer over direct heat.
   (4) Cover with parchment paper; finish cooking over direct heat or in a moderate oven.
   (5) Remove main item; keep warm.
   (6) Prepare a sauce from the cuisson.
   (7) Serve hot, with sauce.
3 Natural juices from the main item and also a possible combination of herbs, vegetables, and sauce are heated inside a parchment bag in a hot oven and become a vapor or steam. Foods are cooked in a steambath in an enclosed environment.
4 (a) Poaching: Temperature range is 160–185°F (70–82°C); little flavor is transferred from the main item into the cooking liquid; items to be poached are naturally tender; cooking liquid contains an acid, along with other flavoring ingredients
   (b) Simmering: Temperature range is 185–200°F (82–85°C); greater transfer of flavor from the main item into the cooking liquid; although some are naturally tender, items to be simmered are likely to be less tender; cooking liquid is well flavored, but doesn't necessarily contain an acid
5 - Flavor development is not the same as dry heat, where foods are allowed to brown.
   - Sharp sauces augment, offset, or bolster boiled items.
   - Significant flavor transfer from meat/poultry to cooking liquid.

- Grains, pasta, potatoes are themselves subtle in flavor.
- Pasta, rice and other grains are often considered "vehicles" for the sauce they hold.

6 (a) More-exercised areas of large animals; mature whole birds; large fish; vegetables.

   (b) Braising cooks slowly, with moist heat; softens fibers and connective tissues; develops rich complex sauce.

7 • Blanched vegetables—cooked just long enough to set colors or make them easy to peel

- Pasta—al dente: can be bitten into easily, but still offers a slight resistance and sense of texture
- Parcooked potatoes—cooked to partial doneness
- Fork-tender meats—cooked to a point at which they slide from a kitchen fork easily
- Fully cooked fish fillet—quite tender, though it still retains its shape and color

8 • Must be done immediately prior to service

- Items tend to be delicate and do not hold well
- Best suited to foods that are portion size or in small pieces

9 Seared or partially cooked before combining with sauce, vegetables, or other garnish in parchment.

10 Nutrients lost readily in water do not leach as rapidly in contact with steam.

11 Differences

   (a) Simmering: Cooking liquid is moving gently; cooking liquid is well-flavored; may be used with naturally tender or slightly less-tender items, including well-exercised cuts of meat

   (b) Boiling: Cooking liquid is vigorously moving; cooking liquid is unflavored, or only salted; may not be used with more-tender items, and is best with dried beans, grains, meals, and vegetables

   Similarities

   They both rehydrate, cook food; ratio of liquid to item being cooked is the same; a tight-fitting lid is occasionally appropriate; and food is completely submerged in cooking liquid.

12 Grain is sautéed briefly in fat, simmered in stock or water, and should be light, fluffy, and relatively dry.

   (1) Smother aromatic vegetables in fat.

   (2) Add the grain and stir until it is coated with the fat.

   (3) Add the correct amount of liquid; bring to a simmer.

   (4) Cover and finish over direct heat or in an oven.

   (5) Fluff with a fork and serve.

13 • Undercooking or braising at high temperature for an insufficient time

- Improper searing
- Failure to remove the lid during final stages
- Sauce not properly reduced or finished

14 • Blanquette

- Bouillabaisse
- Fricassée
- Goulash
- Navarin
- Ragout
- Matelote

Keywords

Al dente (It.): "To the tooth;" to cook an item, such as pasta or vegetables, until it is tender but still firm, not soft.

Blanch; blanched: To cook an item briefly in boiling water or hot fat before finishing or storing it.

Boil; boiling: A cooking method in which items are immersed in liquid at or above the boiling point (212°F/100°C).

Braise; braising: A cooking method in which the main item, usually meat, is seared in fat, then simmered in stock or another liquid in a covered vessel.

En papillote (Fr.): Foods prepared by encasing them in paper and cooking at high enough temperatures to cause steam to build up in the bag.

Fork-tender: A test of doneness for foods; should be easily pierced or cut by a fork, or should slide readily from a fork when lifted.

Fully cooked: Foods cooked completely, as in tender grains, vegetables, or fruits, fork-tender or well-done meats.

Pan-steaming: Cooking foods in a very small amount of liquid in a covered pan over direct heat.

Parcook: To partially cook an item before storing or finishing by another method; may be the same as BLANCHING.

Pilaf: A technique for cooking grains in which the grain is sautéed briefly in butter, then simmered in stock or water with various seasonings. (Also called Pilau, Pilaw, Pullao, Pilav.)

Poach: A method in which items are cooked gently in simmering liquid.

Risotto: A short-grained rice that is sautéed briefly in butter with onions and possibly other aromatics, then combined with stock, which is added in several additions and stirred constantly, producing a creamy texture with grains that are still *al dente*.

Shallow-poach/shallow-poaching: A method in which items are cooked gently in a shallow pan of simmering liquid. The liquid is often reduced and used as the basis of a sauce.

Simmer/simmering: To maintain the temperature of a liquid just below boiling. Also, a cooking method in which items are cooked in simmering liquid.

Spaetzle: A soft noodle or dumpling made from a flour-and-egg batter, simmered in a liquid until done.

Steaming: A cooking method in which items are cooked in a vapor bath created by boiling water or other liquids.

Stew/stewing: A cooking method nearly identical to braising but generally involving smaller pieces of meat and, hence, a shorter cooking time. Stewed items also may be blanched, rather than seared, to give the finished product a pale color. Also, a dish prepared by using the stewing method.

Charcuterie and Garde-Manger

Objectives

- Describe the basic duties of the garde-manger station (pages 401–403)
- Identify the components and preparation techniques for a variety of forcemeats, including:
    Straight (pages 405–407)
    Country-style (pages 407–408)
    Mousseline (pages 408–409)
    Gratin (page 408)
    Emulsified (pages 409–411)
- Explain the purpose of thickeners and binders in forcemeat preparations and name several different types (pages 404–405)
- Describe the purpose and method for using pâté dough in forcemeat preparations (page 405)
- Understand the use and purpose of aspic gelée in forcemeat preparations (page 405)
- Describe a number of garde-manger and charcuterie specialties, including:
    Quenelles (pages 411–412)
    Country-style pâté (pages 412–413)
    Pâté en croûte (pages 413–416)
    Terrines (page 416)
    Sausages (pages 416–418)
    Galantines (pages 418–419)
- Explain different curing methods, as well as special ingredients used to produce cured and smoked foods (pages 419–420)

Lecture Outline

BACKGROUND/HISTORY
FORCEMEATS
  Basic Forcemeat Types
- Straight forcemeats
- Country-style forcemeats
- Gratin forcemeat
- Mousseline
- Emulsified forcemeats

Basic Preparation Guidelines
1. Maintain proper sanitation and temperature at all times.
2. Grind foods properly.
  Progressive Grinding:
   - Cut all solid foods into dice or strips that will fit easily through the grinder's feed tube.
   - Do not force the foods through the feed tube with a tamper.
   - Be sure that the blade is sharp.
   - For all but very delicate meats (fish or some types of organ meats, for example), begin with a die that has large or medium openings. Continue to grind through progressively smaller dies until the correct consistency is achieved.
   - Remember to chill ingredients and equipment between successive grindings.
   - When using a food processor to finish grinding the meat, be sure that the blade is very sharp and that meat is not over-processed.

  Special Preparations and Ingredients
- Thickeners and Binders (Panadas)
- Pâté Dough
- Aspic Gelée
- Curing Salt (TCM)

Straight Forcemeat
  Mise en Place
1. Assemble all ingredients and preparations necessary for a straight forcemeat.
   - Dominant or theme meat
   - Fat

- Panada or other binder
- Seasoning, flavoring, and garnish

Method
1. Have all ingredients and equipment at the correct temperature, under 40°F (4° C).
2. Combine the dominant meat, fat, and (if appropriate) the garnish ingredients with a marinade and refrigerate them.
3. Run the meats and fat through a meat grinder, using a die with large openings (coarse die).
4. Place the ground meat in a food processor and add the panada. Process the mixture to a smooth consistency.
5. Gently fold the garnish into the forcemeat by hand, working over ice.

Country-Style Forcemeat
  Mise en Place
1. Assemble all ingredients and preparations necessary for a country-style forcemeat.
   - Dominant or theme meat
   - Fat
   - Panada or other binder
   - Seasoning, flavoring, and garnish

Method
1. Prepare all meats, fat, and garnish ingredients as indicated by the recipe.
2. Grind the meats once through a coarse die and again through a medium die, and hold over ice or keep them refrigerated.
3. Push the liver through a sieve (tamis) to remove all sinews, membranes, and fibers.
4. Gently work the sieved liver and panada into the ground meats and fat by hand.

Gratin Forcemeat
  Mise en Place
1. Assemble all ingredients and preparations necessary for a gratin forcemeat.
   - Dominant or theme meat
   - Fat
   - Panada or other binder
   - Seasoning, flavoring, and garnish

Method
1. Sear the theme meat first to give it the proper flavor.
2. Grind the other meats, pork fat, and cooked meat through a course die and then through a medium die.
3. Stir the panada into the ground meats, working over ice.

Mousseline Forcemeat
  Mise en Place
  1. Assemble all ingredients and preparations necessary for a mousseline forcemeat.
     • Dominant or theme meat
     • Fat
     • Panada or other binder
     • Seasoning, flavoring, and garnish
  Method
  1. Cut the meat into dice, and keep it very cold until it is time to prepare the forcemeat.
  2. Grind the meat to a paste in a cold food processor.
  3. With the machine running, add cold heavy cream in a thin stream.
  4. Push the forcemeat through a drum sieve to remove any sinews and membranes that may remain.
  5. The forcemeat is ready to be used at this point as a stuffing or to prepare sausages, terrines, or quenelles.

Emulsion or 5/4/3 Forcemeat
  Mise en Place
  1. Assemble all ingredients and preparations necessary for an emulsion forcemeat.
     • Dominant or theme meat
     • Fat
     • Seasoning, flavoring, and garnish
  Method
  1. Cut all meats and fat into dice or strips. Hold the meats and fat separately and keep them very cold.
  2. Add curing salt to the meat only; do not add it to the fat.

3. Grind the meats separately through the fine die once.
4. Grind the fat through a fine die.
5. Make a quenelle to test for binding and taste.

GARDE-MANGER AND CHARCUTERIE SPECIALTIES
Quenelles
  Method
  1. Prepare the forcemeat and keep it chilled until it is time to poach the quenelles.
  2. Bring the poaching liquid to 150°F (65°C).
  3. Shape the quenelles.
  4. Poach the quenelles in the poaching liquid.
  5. When making a sample quenelle, be sure to test it at serving temperature.

Pâté de Campagne/Country-Style Pâté
  Method
  1. Line the mold completely with thin slices of fatback. There should be a 2- to 3-inch overhang on all sides.
  2. Add the garnished country-style forcemeat to the lined mold and press it down with a spatula to remove any air pockets.
  3. Fold the overhanging fatback onto the top of the pâté to completely encase the forcemeat.
  4. Lay various herbs and spices over the top of the pâté, if desired. Place the lid on the mold or cover tightly with foil. Cook the pâté in a bain-marie in order to maintain the correct temperature.
  5. After the pâté has cooked to the correct internal temperature, allow it to cool to room temperature. Pour off all the fat and liquid that may have collected in the mold. Pour aspic gelée into the mold to fill it to the top. Then chill it completely before slicing.

Pâté en Croûte
Method

1. Prepare the forcemeat as necessary, according to the type. Keep forcemeat and garnish cold.
2. Line the mold.
3. Lay the pieces into the mold and press them into place.
4. Use egg wash to "glue" the pastry together in the corners and pinch the seams closed or pinch away the excess in the corners.
5. Line the bottom and sides of the dough-lined mold with sheets of fatback, thinly sliced prosciutto, or other sliced meats.
6. Garnish the forcemeat as desired. Add the forcemeat to the lined mold and press out any air pockets.
7. Fold the fatback, prosciutto, or other sliced meat over the top of the forcemeat. Fold over the pastry dough sheets and trim the top layers.
8. Add the cap piece to seal the pâté, and tuck the edges down into the mold.
9. Cover the pâté with aluminum foil and bake it until it is approximately half done (about 45 minutes). Remove from oven. Remove foil.
10. Using round cutters, cut one or two vent holes in the pastry to allow steam to escape.
11. Complete the baking in a 350°F (170°C) oven to an internal temperature of 150°F (65°C) for meat and 145°F (63°C) for fish and vegetables.
12. Remove the pâté from the oven and let it cool for about an hour. Drain away any cooking liquid. Fill the mold with aspic, pouring the liquid through the holes that have been cut in the crust.
13. Chill the pâté thoroughly before slicing and serving.

Terrines
Method

1. Prepare a forcemeat as desired or necessary according to the recipe. Chill it until it is time to fill the mold.
2. Prepare any garnishes as desired or necessary. Keep them refrigerated until they are ready to be used.
3. Prepare the mold.
4. Fill the mold, adding the garnish as described for pâtés.
5. Fold all liners over the mold's surface.
6. Cover the terrine with its lid.
7. Place the terrine in a roasting pan. Set the pan on the rack of a 300°F (150°C) oven. Add enough boiling water to come up nearly to the level of the top of the forcemeat.
8. Bake the terrine to an internal temperature of 150°F (65°C) for meats and 140°F (60°C) for fish.
9. Remove the terrine from the bath and allow it to cool.
10. If desired, fill the mold with aspic once it has been cooled and the weight has been removed. Chill the terrine thoroughly before slicing and serving it.

Sausages
Method

1. Prepare and garnish the forcemeat as desired or required by the recipe used.
2. Rinse the casings thoroughly in tepid water to remove the salt and to make them more pliable.
3. Be sure that all parts of the sausage stuffer that will come in contact with the forcemeat are clean and chilled.
4. Tie a double knot in the casing end.
5. Gather the casing over the nozzle of the sausage stuffer.
6. Support the casing as the forcemeat is expressed through the nozzle and into the casing.
7. If the sausage is to be made into links, use either of the following methods: Press the casing into links at the desired

intervals and then twist the link in alternating directions for each link; or, tie the casing with twine at the desired intervals.

8. At this point, fresh sausages may be cooked or stored under refrigeration. Other types of sausage may undergo additional curing, smoking, or drying.

Galantines

Method

1. Remove the skin, keeping it as intact as possible.
2. Bone out the dominant meat, reserving intact any pieces that will be used for garnish.
3. Trim the skin to form a large rectangle.
4. Tie the ends with butcher's twine and use a strip of cheesecloth to secure it at even intervals in order to maintain the shape of the cylinder.
5. Place the galantine on a perforated rack and then submerge it in a simmering stock.
6. Let the galantine cool in the cooking liquid.
7. Unwrap the galantine before slicing and serving it.

Cured and Smoked Items

   Cold Smoking

   Hot Smoking

Cured Salmon (Gravad Lox)

   Method

1. Coat trimmed salmon fillets with a dry-cure-and-herb mixture. Wrap tightly in cheesecloth, place in hotel pan, and weight them with a press plate.
2. Drain away any drippings that have accumulated in the pan and reserve them.
3. Unwrap the salmon and scrape away the cure. Slice the salmon very thinly on the diagonal to serve.
4. Prepare a mayonnaise using the reserved drippings to season (optional).

Daube

Method

1. Gently simmer the meats in an aromatic broth enriched with vegetables and herbs. Once the meats are tender, trim and cut them into julienne or dice.
2. Line the mold, usually an earthenware terrine, with plastic wrap.
3. Place the prepared meats, along with the desired herbs and other garnishes, in the mold.
4. Fold back the overhanging plastic wrap over the top of the mold to seal the daube, and refrigerate the entire dish until the aspic is firmly set.
5. Once the daube is thoroughly chilled, it is ready to be sliced and served.

SUMMARY

Discussion Topics

TOPIC: Benefits of making sausage in-house
- Low food cost
- Flavor
- Availability (merguez, chorizo, etc.)
- Total utilization
- Signature sausage

TOPIC: Cold sauces used in garde manger
- Coulis
- Mayonnaise base
- Vinaigrette
- Thickened sauces
- Coating sauces, chaud-froid
- Dairy based
- Marinades
- Miscellaneous
   Compote
   Relishes
   Chutneys
   Fruit butters
   Salsas

Resource: Books

Classical Cooking the Modern Way, 2nd ed. Eugen Pauli. Van Nostrand Reinhold. New York, 1989.

Escoffier: The Complete Guide to the Art of Modern Cookery. Auguste Escoffier. Van Nostrand Reinhold. New York, 1995.

TOPIC: Banquet Plating
- BUFF: Balance, Uniformity, Flow, Function

TOPIC: Gelatin: Making aspic
- Classic method
    Flavorful stock
    Clarification
    Add gelatin, if necessary
- Quick method
    Consomme
    Add commercial gelatin
- Powdered method
    Instant aspic on the market
    Save time but sacrifice quality
    Agar Agar—"Vegetarian" gelatin, made from seaweed

TOPIC: Composed salads
- Greens, legumes, vegetables
- Main item
- Dressing
- Garnishes

TOPIC: Composed salads: balancing flavors and textures
- Hot, warm and cold, frozen
- Sweet and sour, tart
- Soft, tender and crisp
- Spicy and cooling
- Lean and rich, fatty

Resource: Book

Lettuce in Your Kitchen. Chris Schlesinger and John Willoughby. William Morrow. New York, 1996.

TOPIC: Side salads/green salads
- See Chapter 6, Mise en Place, for cleaning information

TOPIC: Appetizers: importance in menu development
- Signature appetizers are customer "draws". Jeffrey Buben, at Vidalia, Washington, D.C., always offers a whole baked Vidalia onion.
- Amuse-geule—a "tidbit" offered "gratis" by the chef as customers look over the menu.
- Other "freebies" offered in restaurants include: chips and salsa, fried wonton noodles, eggplant caviar.
- Poo-poo, antipasta, and zakushi platters are all platters meant to be shared (nachos and large sampler platters are popular in "family-style" restaurants).

TOPIC: Contemporary and ethnic reception food, hors d'oeuvres, and appetizers
- Antipasto (Italian)
- Tapas (Spanish)
- Mezzes (Greek)
- Dim sum (Chinese)
- Bruschetta, crostini, focaccia, pizza (Italian)
- Crackers, flatbreads, crisps (Scandinavian)
- Canapes/fingerfood (American/English)
    Main item
    Spread
    Sauce
    Garnish

TOPIC: Cold soups as appetizers
- Fruit
- Vegetable

TOPIC: "High-end" garde-manger items
- Caviar
    Domestic
    Imported
    Other roes
    Service
- Smoked salmon
- Foie gras

The Production of Foie Gras. *Culinary Institute of America*, 1995.

Preparing Foie Gras. *Culinary Institute of America*, 1995.

TOPIC: Forcemeats: production/preparation and Service

- Safety (temperature control, equipment, other)
- Developing best flavor and texture (establish emulsion, spices, making test quenelles)
- Plating and presentation (classic garnish and sauce)

    Combinations such as cumberland sauce with poultry-based galantine, mustards, and pickled items with pork-based terrines and pâtés.

    Contemporary renditions such as red pepper and eggplant terrine on a salad of wild greens, seafood sausage grilled on foccacia.

Resource: Magazines

Chef
Food Arts
ArtCulinaire
Food and Wine
Bon Appetit

Additional material for this chapter may be found in the back of this manual. See the charts on sausage grinding.

Assignments

1 The mayonnaise keeps breaking while it is being prepared. How can this be avoided? How can this be repaired?
- The egg yolks and oil must be the same temperature.
- The oil must be poured slowly.
- Repair by starting the emulsion over with water and mustard and maybe another egg yolk.

- If you are working in a very hot or very cold area, you may need to move to area where temperature is less extreme.

2 The salad dressing is always in a big pool on the plate and the greens seem wilted. What has happened?
- The dressing may be too thin. An emulsifier, such as mustard or egg yolk, might help.
- The lettuce may not have been dried adequately, which would also "thin out" the dressing and prevent it from adhering to greens.
- Too much dressing may have been applied —this is a frequent mistake in American restaurants.
- The salad may have been dressed too early. This will cause the greens to wilt.
- Dressing may have been ladled over salad, rather than properly mixing/tossing in a large bowl.
- See also pages 229–231.

3 The arugula salad is crunchy and gritty. Why?
- The arugula was not washed properly. It should have been washed in a sink repeatedly until there was no grit visible on the bottom of the sink.
- See also pages 229–231.

4 After cooling the galantine, it is ready to be sliced, but the slices crumble. Why?
- The galantine was overcooked.
- The proper amount of panada was not added.
- The emulsion wasn't done properly.
- See also pages 418–419.
- See also Thickeners and Binders, pages 404–405.

5 The outdoor reception will be 3 hours long. The pâtés and terrines are to be plated on large china platters. Temperatures are expected to be in the 80°s. How would you handle this?
- Take a limited number of platters outside at a time and use smaller platters, if possible.
- If possible, lay the platters over large ice-filled trays.

- Try to make sure the reception tables are under open-sided tents to get air flow and shade.
- If labor cost allows, "butler" any "delicate" foods so they will not be sitting out.
- See also pages 44–45.

6 The garde-manger was in a hurry and forgot to put a chimney in his pâté en croûte. What might happen?
- Steam might build up and cause the crust to rupture.
- There would be no opening to pour in the aspic.
- See also Pâté en Croûte, pages 413–416.

7 Give a number of examples of foods not normally served as appetizers that may be served as such, or as canapes, or hors d' oeurves, and explain what modifications, if any, might be necessary.
- Tacos, tortillas, quiches, pizzas, sandwiches —all made in miniature
- Frittatas, pizzas, sandwiches—cut to size
- Vegetables, roasted, grilled, marinated—cut to size and/or skewered
- Almost any entrée can be served as a plated appetizer by reducing the portion size. Pastas and fish dishes are often popular as appetizers for people not willing to "commit" to an entrée sized portion.
- See also pages 690–696.

8 How has the role of salads changed in the United States over the last several years? Can this change be seen as coming from any particular region of the country? If so, where and why?
- Salads are perceived as "healthy" and so have become more popular (even when they are not so healthy, such as at the fat-ladden salad bars).
- Salads are no longer a wedge of iceberg lettuce. Flavorful produce is available almost everywhere now.
- California is most responsible for growing, demanding, and receiving good-quality produce.

Alice Waters
Boutique farming
Organic farming
- See also pages 16–17, 64–65.

9 What can be done to prepare salad dressings that have a creamy appearance and mouth-feel without relying on egg yolks (as there is growing concern over salmonellosis associated with the consumption of raw eggs)?
- Pasteurized egg yolks are available
- Reduced or thickened vegetable juices or chicken stock (chilled), buttermilk, and evaporated skim milk are all ingredients which can supply a somewhat similar mouth-feel
- Add or increase the amount of mustard
- Purées of vegetables or herbs

10 Today's consumer is more likely to be concerned about reducing overall fat, cholesterol, and sodium in the diet. Discuss some modifications to hors d'oeuvres, appetizers, charcuterie, and garde-manger items to make them appealing without relying on standard formulas that might be too heavy, salty, or fatty for contemporary palates.
- Smaller portions with sides of grains or greens
- Red meats can often be replaced by white meats or fish in terrines, pâtés, and sausages.
- Accompanying sauces can be made lighter, lower in fat (see Question 10). This also applies to pasta appetizers.
- More salads can be offered
- Sharp or pungent cheese used sparingly can add flavor without much fat.
- See also pages 79, 418–19.

11 There are specific functions perfomed by some of the items used in traditional charcuterie items. Salt and fat are good examples. What are their functions, and how has modern technology lessened their importance?
- Salt and fat were both used as preservatives. They allowed the meat to be held without refrigeration. We no longer rely on salt and fat because we have refrigeration. With a few

exceptions (proscuitto, country ham, confit), these ingredients are used primarily for flavor now.

- Spices were also used to mask flavor of "high" meats that were held for extended periods without benefit of refrigeration.
- See also pages 401–403.

Answer Key to Self-Study Questions

1 • Charcuterie: products, typically cured, brined, and/or smoked—sausages, smoked hams, bacon, pates, terrines, and head cheeses, to preserve them.
   • Garde-manger or "cold kitchen": the preparation of cold appetizers, soups, salads, and buffet and reception items.

2 (1) To reduce the risk of contamination.
   (2) To preserve the quality of the product.

3 (a) Meat is passed through a grinder a number of times with successively smaller die fittings to produce a smoothly ground product.
   (b) Helps to ensure a proper emulsion and texture in the finished forcemeat.

4 • Bread panada—bread soaked in milk
   • Flour panada—a heavy béchamel
   • Pâté à choux
   • Rice- or potato-based panadas
   • Liaison of heavy cream and eggs to ensure that item does not fall apart or crumble when sliced.

5 (a) Prepared from a well-seasoned stock, which is perfectly clarified and highly gelatinous, often strengthened with additional gelatin.
   (b) Applied to foods while it is still warm; creates a protective coating; prevent items from drying out.

6 Sear the theme meat, cool; progressively grind other meats with seared meat; stir a panada into the ground meats; test for quality; use in desired application.

7 Derives from an old French word, *galin,* mean-

ing "chicken." Originally made from poultry and game birds; stuffed and tied in the bird's natural shape.

8 Allows the chef to test the forcemeat for flavor, texture, color, and consistency.
   (1) Heat some poaching liquid to a bare simmer, about 150°F (65°C).
   (2) Shape the quenelles.
   (3) Poach the quenelles.
   (4) Allow the quenelle to cool completely before tasting.

9 (a) Also known as TCM (Tinted Curing Mixture); tinted pink to avoid mistaking it for regular salt; combination of 94% salt and 6% sodium nitrate.
   (b) Primary function is to prevent botulism in forcemeat items that are to undergo lengthy smoking at extremely low temperatures, and to produce a pink color in sausages, pâtés, and other items.

10 • Fatback
   • Blanched romaine leaves
   • Leek leaves
   • Blanched vegetables
   • Thin slices of ham or smoked fish
   • Plastic wrap

11 (1) Fill the terrine and cover with a lid.
   (2) Cook in the oven in a hot water bath.
   (3) Bake to an appropriate internal temperature.
   (4) Remove terrine from the water bath and allow to cool.
   (5) Weight and refrigerate.
   (6) (Optional) fill the terrine with aspic and chill again.
   (7) Slice and serve directly from the mold.

12 • Preparation of a variety of meats, usually including the tongue, head, and feet of veal and/or pork.
   • Slowly braising the meats, slicing or cutting the meats, placing in a mold, adding cooking liquid, allowing daube to cool into a gel firm enough to slice.

13 (1) Coat salmon fillet with a dry-cure-and-herb mixture.

(2) Wrap tightly in cheesecloth.

(3) Place in a hotel pan, weight with a press plate, and allow to cure for anywhere from several hours to several days.

(4) Drain away any drippings.

(5) Unwrap the salmon and scrape away the cure.

(6) Thinly slice salmon.

(7) Prepare mayonnaise-style sauce with the drippings, if desired, and serve.

Keywords

Aspic gelée (Fr.): A clear jelly made from stock (or occasionally from fruit or vegetable juices) thickened with gelatin. Used to coat foods or cubed and used as a garnish.

Binder: An ingredient or appareil used to thicken a sauce or hold together another mixture of ingredients.

Cold smoking: Preparing brined and/or cured foods in a smoker; temperatures are kept at less than 100°F (37°C).

Country-style *(pâté de campagne):* A forcemeat that is coarse in texture, usually made from pork, pork fat, liver, and various garnishes.

Curing salt: A mixture of 94 percent table salt (sodium chloride) and 6 percent sodium nitrite used to preserve meats. (Also known as Tinted Curing Mixture, or TCM.)

Daube: A meat stew braised in red wine, traditionally in a daubière, a specialized casserole with a tight-fitting lid and indentations to hold hot coals. In charcutière: a preparation of a variety of meats that is slowly simmered then chilled until the proteins of the meat set the cooking liquid into a gel firm enough to slice.

Emulsified (emulsion) forcemeat (5/4/3): A forcemeat in which meats and fat are carefully brought into a state of emulsion, with strict adherence to temperature controls to ensure a perfectly homogenous end product.

Forcemeat: A mixture of chopped or ground meat and other ingredients used for pâtés, sausages, and other preparations.

Galantine: Boned meat (usually poultry) that is stuffed, rolled, poached, and served cold, usually in aspic.

Gratin forcemeat: A mixture of meats and fat in which the garnish meat is first seared and cooled before being incorporated.

Gravad lox/gravlax: Salmon cured for several days in a combination of sugar, salt, and herbs.

Hot smoking: The process of preparing foods in a smokehouse (after they have been cured or brined) at temperatures above 145°F (63°C).

Mousseline (forcemeat) (Fr.): A mousse; a sauce made by folding whipped cream into hollandaise; or a very light forcemeat based on white meat or seafood lightened with cream and eggs.

Nitrites/nitrates: Chemical substances used to preserve foods, found especially in cured meats and TCM (Tinting Curing Mix, or curing salt).

Panada: An appareil based on starch (such as flour or crumbs), moistened with a liquid, that is used as a binder.

Pâté (Fr.): A rich forcemeat of meat, game, poultry, seafood, and/or vegetables, baked in pastry or in a mold or dish.

Pâté dough: A lean dough used to line a pâté mold, for pâté en croûte.

Pâté en croûte: Pâté baked in a pastry crust.

Progressive grinding: The procedure of grinding foods through successively smaller die in order to create a good emulsion between lean and fat ingredients.

Quenelle (Fr.): A light, poached dumpling based on a forcemeat (usually chicken, veal, seafood, or game) bound with eggs that is shaped in an oval by using two spoons.

Sausage: A forcemeat mixture shaped into patties or links; typically highly seasoned.

Straight forcemeat: A forcemeat combining pork and pork fat with another meat in equal parts that is made by grinding the mixture together.

Terrine: A loaf of forcemeat, similar to a pâté, but cooked in a covered mold in a bain-marie. Also, the mold used to cook such items, usually an oval shape made of ceramic.

Wet cure: A curing process in which foods are completely submerged in a brine or marinade.

Baking and Pastry

Objectives

- Describe the function of each of the primary ingredient groups used in baking (pages 426–429)
- Differentiate chemical, organic, and physical leaveners and explain the way that each works and the typical fashion in which each is used (pages 427–428)
- List and explain the basic pieces of equipment used in a bakeshop (pages 429–430)
- Explain the mise en place, mixing, shaping, and baking methods for each of the following types of baked goods:

    quick breads, cakes, and other batters (pages 436–442)

    pastry doughs for pies and pastries (pages 442–446)

    roll-in doughs (pages 446–450)

    creams, Bavarians, and mousses (pages 451–456)

    sauces and glazes (pages 456–457)

    frozen desserts (pages 457–458)

    simple cookies, candies, and confections (pages 458–460)
- Understand decorating techniques for pastries and cakes, and know how to use a variety of special tools for this purpose (pages 461–465)

Lecture Outline

TOPIC: Baking Mise en Place and Yeast Doughs

THE FUNCTION OF BASIC INGREDIENTS IN BAKING

Baking ingredients will generally fall into six basic categories of function:

- strengtheners, such as flour and eggs
- shorteners, such as butters and oils
- sweeteners, including a variety of sugars and syrups
- chemical and organic leaveners
- thickeners, such as cornstarch, flour, and eggs
- a number of different flavorings

Strengtheners

Shorteners

Sweeteners

Leaveners

    Chemical Leaveners

    Organic Leaveners

Yeast
Sourdough Starter
Physical Leaveners
Thickeners
Arrowroot and cornstarch
Flour
Eggs
Gelatin
Flavorings

TECHNIQUES USED TO PREPARE INGREDIENTS AND EQUIPMENT
Scaling
Sifting Dry Ingredients
Selecting and Preparing Pans and Molds
Selecting and Preparing Ovens

YEAST-RAISED BREADS
Mixing Yeast Doughs
Mise En Place
1. Assemble and prepare all ingredients.
2. Assemble all the necessary equipment.
Method
1. Blend the fresh yeast with some or all of the liquid and mix until it is evenly blended. Instant dry yeast should be thoroughly blended with the dry ingredients before adding liquids.
2. Add all the remaining ingredients—except the salt—to the yeast mixture. Once all the dry ingredients have been added, add the salt on top of them.
3. Mix on low speed until the dough starts to "catch." It should look like a shaggy mass at this point.
4. Increase the mixing speed to medium and continue to knead until the dough develops a smooth appearance and feels springy when touched.
5. Remove the dough to a clean bowl that has been lightly oiled. Cover the dough with plastic wrap and let it rise.
6. When the dough has risen sufficiently, punch it down.
7. Remove the dough to a prepared work surface.

Shaping Doughs
The Final Rise/Pan-Proofing
Docking Breads and Rolls
Baking Yeast Breads
Cooling and Storing Yeast Breads

TOPIC: Batters
QUICK BREADS, CAKES, AND OTHER BATTERS
• The *straight mixing method* calls for all ingredients to be combined at once and blended into a batter.
• The *creaming method* is used to prepare products with more refined crumb and texture—pound cakes, butter cakes, and most drop cookies.
• The *"two-stage"* method is used to prepare cakes that contain a very high percentage of sugar. The dry ingredients are first blended with all of the shortening and half of the liquid until smooth, then the remaining wet ingredients are gradually added.
• The *foaming method,* which produces the lightest texture, is used for génoise (sponge cakes), angel food, and chiffon cakes.

The Straight Mixing Method
Mise en Place
1. Assemble all ingredients required for the batter.
Method
1. Sift together all of the dry ingredients, and have them ready.
2. Combine all the liquid or pourable ingredients (eggs, milk or buttermilk, oil, or melted butter, for example) in a mixing bowl. Blend well.
3. Combine the dry ingredients with the liquid ingredients all at once.
4. Scale off the batter into prepared baking pans.
5. Bake the batter at the appropriate temperature until it is baked through.
6. Remove the item from the oven, then cool it on racks before serving and/or storing.

The Creaming Method

Mise en Place

1. Assemble all ingredients required for the batter.

Method

1. Combine the butter (or other shortening) and sugar and blend them together until the mixture is smooth, light, and creamy.
2. Gradually add the eggs, which should be at room temperature.
3. Once the eggs are incorporated, add the sifted dry ingredients, alternating with the liquid ingredients.
4. Pour the batter into pans that have been greased and floured or lined with parchment paper. Bake the batter until the cake springs back when pressed lightly with a fingertip and the edges have begun to shrink from the pan's sides.
5. Remove the cake from the oven, and cool it properly before serving and/or storing.

The Two-Stage Method

Mise en Place

1. Assemble all ingredients required for the batter.

Method

1. Place all of the sifted dry ingredients in the bowl of a mixer.
2. Add all of the shortening and approximately half of the liquid to the dry ingredients, and mix them using the paddle attachment, at a low speed.
3. Combine the eggs with the remaining liquid ingredients and blend them into the batter, in two or three parts using the whip attachment.
4. After all of the wet ingredients have been incorporated, increase the speed of the mixer to medium and mix the batter for another 3 minutes.
5. Scale the batter as desired and place it into prepared pans. Bake the cake at an appropriate temperature, usually 350°F (175°C).

The Foaming Method

Mise en Place

1. Assemble all ingredients required for the batter. If you are using egg whites as the foundation of a cake, be sure that they are completely free of all traces of yolk.

Method

1. Combine the eggs (whole, yolk, or whites) with sugar in a bowl. Place the bowl over a hot-water bath and heat it to approximately 100°F (38°C), whipping constantly.
2. Remove the mixture from the heat and beat it with the whip attachment until the eggs form a stable foam that has tripled in volume.
3. Gently fold in the sifted dry ingredients.
4. Add any flavorings or additional ingredients at this point.
5. Immediately pour the batter into pans that have been correctly prepared.
6. Remove the cake from the oven and let it cool.

MIXING METHODS FOR OTHER BATTERS AND DOUGHS

Biscuits, Scones, and Soda Breads

TOPIC: Pastry Doughs

PASTRY DOUGH

Basic Pie Dough

Mise en Place

1. Assemble all ingredients.
2. Assemble all equipment necessary.

Method

1. Combine the flour and the fat.
2. Add the cold water all at once; mix it quickly into the flour-and-fat mixture.
3. Gather the dough into a smooth ball and chill it until it is firm.
4. Turn the chilled dough onto a floured work surface. Scale the dough into the correct size.
5. Using even strokes, roll the dough into the desired thickness and shape. Turn it occasionally to produce an even shape

and to keep it from sticking to the work surface.

Preparing Pies And Tarts

Lining a Pie Plate or Tart Mold

Baking Blind

Fillings For Pies And Tarts

Topping Pies And Tarts

Baking Pies And Tarts

ROLL-IN DOUGHS

Mise en Place

1. Assemble all ingredients necessary to prepare the dough.
2. Assemble all equipment necessary.

Methods for Doughs with Separate Roll-ins

1. Working on a floured surface, roll the prepared dough out into a rectangle, about ½-inch thick.
2. Roll out the roll-in between two pieces of parchment paper to form a rectangle that will cover two-thirds of the dough; it should be the same approximate thickness (½-inch) and consistency as the dough.
3. Position the roll-in on the dough so that one-third of the dough is uncovered and there is a ½-inch border on the other three sides. Fold the uncovered third of the dough over the roll-in. Next, fold the opposite third on top of the dough. The dough should appear stacked in the five layers, alternating layers of dough and roll-in. Use your fingertips to weld the seams together.

Once the roll-in has been encased in the dough, it is rolled out and given a three- or letter-fold. This initial fold is then followed with the recommended number of three or four folds. Be sure to brush away any excess flour from the dough. Left on the dough, this flour might interfere with proper layer formation. Once the dough has received all the necessary turns, it should be allowed to rest under refrigeration overnight before rolling, shaping, and baking.

Sidebar Handling Roll-In Doughs

Method for Blitz Puff Pastry

Rolling, Folding, and Shaping the Finished Dough

1. Roll the dough out into a rectangle, and fold the dough into thirds (a letter-fold). If the dough has warmed up, stop at this point and let the dough firm in the refrigerator.
2. Turn the dough so that the longest edge is parallel to the edge of the work surface. Roll the dough out again into a rectangle, and make a "book-fold" as follows:

Fold the narrow edges of the rectangle in until they meet in the center of the rectangle. Now fold the rectangle in half again. Repeat the book-fold another three or four times, allowing the dough sufficient time to firm between rolling out the dough and folding it.

Handling Method for Phyllo Dough

Fillings for Pastries

Pâte à Choux

Mise en Place

1. Assemble and prepare all ingredients
2. Assemble all equipment.

Method

1. Bring the liquid and butter to a full boil. Add the flour and cook it until the mixture pulls away from the pan, forming a ball.
2. Place the dough in the bowl of a mixer. Use the paddle attachment to mix it for a few minutes, allowing the dough to cool slightly.
3. Add the eggs gradually, in three or four additions, working the dough until it is smooth each time, scraping down the bowl's sides and bottom until all the eggs are incorporated.
4. The dough is ready to use at this point. It should be piped onto sheet pans lined with parchment paper, according to the desired result.

5. To properly bake pâte à choux, begin the baking process at a high temperature (375 to 400°F/190 to 204°C). Reduce the heat to 250°F (120°C) once the pâte à choux begins to take on color. Continue to bake until golden brown and there are no visible beads of moisture on their exteriors.

TOPIC: Creams, Bavarians, and Mousses

Vanilla Sauce

Mise en Place

1. Assemble all ingredients for the sauce.
2. Assemble all equipment necessary to prepare the sauce.

Method

1. Combine the eggs with half of the sugar in a stainless steel bowl. Blend them well, using a whip.
2. Combine the milk with half of the sugar in a large pot and heat it just to the boiling point. If you are using a vanilla bean to flavor the sauce, it should be added now, to steep in the milk as it heats.
3. Temper the egg-and-sugar mixture with the hot milk, return it to the pot. Continue to cook the sauce over low heat until it begins to thicken. Stir the sauce constantly to prevent it from overcooking. The sauce should never come to a boil, because egg yolks and whites coagulate well below the boiling point. The sauce's temperature should not go above 180°F (82°C).
4. Add any desired flavoring ingredients at this point.
5. Once the sauce has reached the correct consistency, strain it immediately through a fine chinois or cheesecloth into a bain-marie or other container set in an ice-water bath. Placing a small amount of melted butter or plastic wrap directly on the sauce's surface will help prevent a skin from forming.

Pastry Cream

Mise en Place

1. Assemble all ingredients required for pastry cream.
2. Assemble all equipment required for pastry cream.

Method

1. Mix the flour, half of the sugar, and the whole eggs together in one bowl and blend them to a smooth consistency.
2. Bring the milk and the remaining sugar to a boil. If a vanilla bean is used to flavor the sauce, it may be added at this point.
3. Use part of the milk mixture to temper the egg mixture. Return the tempered eggs to the pot and continue to cook the mixture until it reaches a full boil. Stir or whip the pastry cream constantly.
4. After removing the pastry cream from the heat, add flavorings and whole butter. Remove the cream to a clean pot and cool it quickly over an ice bath.

Preparing Dessert Soufflés

Bavarian Creams

Mousse

Buttercreams

Two Basic Methods

• A pastry cream or vanilla sauce is prepared, flavored, and allowed to cool. Softened butter is whipped into this base.
• A syrup is made by heating sugar and water. The hot syrup is beaten into eggs (whole, yolks, or whites) to make a meringue or foam, and then softened butter is added gradually.

TOPIC: Sauces, Glazes and Frozen Desserts

Chocolate Sauce

Fondant

Syrups and Glazes

Fruit Sauces

Caramel/Butterscotch Sauces

Sabayon (Zabaglione)

Fruit Curds

FROZEN DESSERTS
Frozen Soufflés and Mousses
Ice Cream and Gelato
Sorbets and Sherbets
Granité

TOPIC: Cookies, Candies, and Dessert Assembly, Plating and Presentation
SIMPLE COOKIES, CANDIES, AND CONFECTIONS
Preparing Cookies, Petits Fours, and Other Small Pastries
Tempering Chocolate for Coating
Method

1. Chop the chocolate coarsely with a chef's knife and place it in a stainless steel bowl. Place the bowl over very low heat or barely simmering water, making sure that no moisture comes in contact with the chocolate. Stir the chocolate occasionally as it melts to keep it at an even temperature throughout.
2. Continue to heat the chocolate until it reaches a temperature of between 105 to 110°F (40 to 43°C).
3. Remove the chocolate from the heat. Add a large piece of unmelted chocolate and stir it in until the temperature drops to approximately 87 to 92°F (30 to 33°C). If the chocolate drops below 85°F (29°C) while working with it, it will be necessary to repeat the steps described here to retemper it.

Preparing Candies from Fondant
SPECIAL TOOLS AND TECHNIQUES FOR DECORATING PASTRIES AND CAKES (DESSERT ASSEMBLY, PLATING, AND PRESENTATION)
Techniques used to create a variety of cakes, tortes.

- Each item must be of high quality, in terms of taste, texture, and appearance.
- All of the elements on the plate or in the pastry should work together to produce a pleasing effect.
- Contrasting textures, colors, and flavors can be successfully combined, but the overall effect should be pleasing, not jarring.

Parchment Cones

1. Fold a sheet of parchment paper on the diagonal, slightly overlapping. Do not form a perfect triangle.
2. Hold the uneven corner between the thumb and forefinger of one hand. Use the other thumb and forefinger to make a "pivot point" by holding the parchment at the diagonal's midpoint.
3. Roll the parchment into a funnel shape, keeping the point closed as the paper is rolled. This may require some practice. It is important to keep the paper taut as it is rolled.
4. When the entire triangle has been rolled into a cone, there will be three points at the cone's top. Fold the point on the outside so that it is on the interior of the cone.
5. Hold the cone so that the tip is pointing downward, and fill the cone slightly more than half full. Fold the outer points in toward the cone's center and fold the last corner over the top of the other points, sealing the cone completely.
6. Hold the cone so that the tip is resting on a cutting surface and use a sharp knife to nick away a small amount of the paper, creating a small opening. The deeper the cut, the larger the opening and, therefore, the larger the lines of piping will be.

Pastry Bags and Tips

1. Select the desired tip and position it securely in the pastry bag's opening.
2. Fold down the bag's top to create a cuff, then transfer the buttercream or other preparation to the bag with a spatula or spoon.
3. Press on the bag first to expel any air pockets. With one hand, press the buttercream down and out of the bag. Use the other hand to support and guide the bag.
4. Remove all the excess buttercream or other filling or frosting from the bag and wash it carefully with warm, soapy water after each use.

Assembling and Decorating Tortes
1. Prepare all the basic components and have them at the correct temperature.
2. To separate a cake into layers, use a knife with a long blade to cut the cake horizontally.
3. Moisten the layers with simple syrup or brush them with melted jam or preserves. Place the first layer on a cake circle, or in the bottom of a round mold.
   If desired, you can cut additional pieces to line the walls of the mold.
4. Spread the filling evenly on each layer, building the cake as you go. You may use a Bavarian cream, a mousse, pastry cream, or custard. Add garnish or flavoring ingredients, such as poached or fresh fruit, as you work.
5. Once the final layer has been added and smoothed off, a glaze or topping should be applied evenly.
Sidebar Decorating Tips for Tortes and Cakes

Discussion Topics

TOPIC: Benefits/disadvantages of preparing breads/desserts in-house

Benefit:	Disadvantage:
Cost	Special equipment
Freshness	Hire baker or train other staff
Quick breads (easy)	Scheduling baking needs around "hot kitchen" needs

TOPIC: Breads, desserts and doughs made in-house vs. convenience foods or made in-house using partially prepped convenience foods (offering the appearance of "homemade" with the convenience of store bought)
- Puff pastry
- Phyllo
- Pie crust
- Pizza dough
- Par-prepped Danish, etc.

TOPIC: Lowfat, healthy dessert ideas

Resource: Magazines

Eating Well
Cooking Light

Resource: Book

Techniques of Healthy Cooking. Culinary Institute of America. Mary Donovan, ed. Van Nostrand Reinhold. New York, 1993.

TOPIC: New ideas for dessert
- Creating signature desserts
- Using more unusual ingredients, herbs and spices.
- Ethnic desserts, e.g. Asian ices, tropical flavors
- Contemporary desserts

Resource: Magazines

ArtCulinaire
Chef
Food Arts

Resource: Organization

U.S. Pastry Alliance
3042 Parkside Dr.
Jenisson, MI 49428
(888) A-Pastry
(616) 669-8112

Resource: Videos

Bread and Baker: From the Source. *Culinary Institute of America,* 1994.
   Tape I—Traditions of French Bread Baking.
   Tape II—Baguettes and Pain de Campagne.
   Tape III—Specialty Breads.

TOPIC: Ethnic Breads
- Current popularity
- Use on a menu
- Pairing with food
- Benefits

Resource: Book

Flatbreads and Flavors. Jeffrey Alford and Naomi Duguid. William Morrow. New York, 1995.

Additional material for this chapter may be found in the back of this manual. See the charts on roll-in doughs

Assignments

1 The students in the bakeshop are having a bad day. Explain why the following problems (A-H) happened and how they can be avoided in the future.

A. A Bavarian cream made with gelatin did not properly set, and there is a tough, rubbery, grainy layer at the bottom of the mold.
   - The gelatin was not properly "bloomed."
   - Next time the gelatin should be softened in a cool liquid ("bloom"), then heated to melt the crystals, before being added.
   - See also pages 428, 453, 744.

B. An experiment was made to adapt a cake formula to meet the needs of a special diet. The end result was a tough, rubbery cake that had no noticeable crumb. Suggest alternatives.
   - The recipe had too little sugar and shortening.
   - Sugar attracts moisture, so adding more sugar will make a more moist and tender product.
   - Shorteners (fats) break the long strands of gluten in the flour and develop a crumb.
   - Use dried or fresh fruit purées to replace fat and add moisture.
   - Use foaming method for cake and brush with a simple syrup.

C. The bread is flat, with a coarse grain, and a thick crust.
   - Might have used a low-gluten flour. If low-gluten flours, such as rye, oat and pum-

pernickel are used, they need to be supplemented with some wheat flour for proper dough development.
   - The yeast may have been old. The yeast should be proofed before using.
   - The yeast may have been added to too hot of a liquid. Test the temperature before using.
   - The dough may have been underkneaded or overkneaded. Proper kneading is essential for the development of the gluten. Determination of how much kneading is necessary will come with experience.
   - The dough may not have had sufficient time to rise.
   - It may have been cooked at too high of a heat, which will cause the outside to cook faster than the inside.
   - See also pages 427–428, 433.

D. The bread tastes fine, but it became stale very quickly after baking.
   - The bread was not allowed to cool before it was covered and stored.
   - It should be cooled completely and covered loosely at room temperature.
   - Lean doughs with no or little fat stale quickly; this is normal.
   - See also page 436.

E. The finished bread did not have the proper volume and is crumbly after baking. It went stale very quickly, too.
   - The yeast may have been old. The yeast should be proofed before using.
   - The yeast may have been added to too hot of a liquid. Test the temperature before using.
   - The dough may have been underkneaded or overkneaded. Proper kneading is essential for the development of the gluten. Determination of how much kneading is necessary will come with experience.
   - The dough may not have had sufficient time to rise.
   - The bread was not allowed to cool before it was covered and stored.

- It should be cooled completely and covered loosely at room temperature.
- See also pages 427–428, 433, 436.

F. A blueberry cake tastes fine, but all of the berries are on the bottom of the cake.
  - The blueberries are too heavy for the cake batter to hold in suspension.
  - Smaller blueberries could be used.
  - Tossing the blueberries in flour before adding to the dough will help them stay in place.

G. A layer cake has large air pockets and uneven rise.
  - It might have been undermixed.
  - It may not have been cooked at the correct temperature.
  - See also pages 437–439.

H. The pie dough is very tough, both before and after it is baked.
  - It was probably overworked.
  - The shortening may not have been chilled.
  - The shortening should be chilled and just briefly worked into the flour.
  - See also pages 426–427, 442–444.

2 In the hotel's pastry kitchen, many of the prepared items are not up to standard. Again, explain why the problems outlined below (A-C) might have occurred, ways to correct them, and ways to avoid them in the future.

A. The apple pie featured on the menu is always prepared by one of the line cooks. She went on vacation and while she was away the pantry cook baked the pies. The crust was soaked on the bottom.
  - The filling may have been too loose. Add flour, cornstarch, tapioca, reduce sugar slightly, or use a different type of apple.
  - The pie may have been undercooked or cooked at too low of a temperature
  - The pie may have been overfilled, causing the juices to overflow and seep under the crust.
  - Strain the filling, or use a thickener.
  - Cook at proper temperature.

- Use toasted bread crumbs on the bottom.
- See also page 445.

B. The pastry chef has prepared a poached pear dessert by gently poaching the fruit in a sugar syrup. The pear is almost crunchy after poaching.
  - Excess sugar in poaching liquid prevents fruit from softening. Use less sugar or try a fruit juice or cider instead of simple syrup.
  - The pear may be undercooked. The timing should be such that the pear is not too hard, but not too soft, either.
  - Cool the pears in the cooking liquid. This will complete the cooking process and the pears will absorb some of the flavors lost to the cooking liquid.
  - See also pages 383–386, 729.

C. The custard sauce is very thick and has an "eggy" flavor.
  - Maybe too many eggs were added.
  - The sauce was not cooked enough.
  - No additional flavoring was added.
  - Use fewer yolks, or add some whole eggs.
  - See also pages 451–452.

3 A pancake batter was prepared in the morning and then left on a shelf over the griddle by the breakfast cook. By the end of the breakfast service period, the pancakes were flat and not as fluffy as those made earlier in the day.
  - The batter may have been overworked.
  - Most likely the heat of the griddle affected the baking powder.
  - A small portion of batter should be held near the griddle. The remaining batter should be kept under refrigeration to keep it wholesome.
  - See also page 427.

4 Breads are among the most basic of foods, but the bread we are most familiar with, yeast-raised breads, took time to evolve. What is the history of breadmaking?
  - Wheat flour wasn't used until the Egyptians.
  - Only low-gluten flours were used except in areas of the world (e.g., Egypt) where wheat flourished.

- High-heat, quick-burning, small ovens were used to conserve fuel. This was great for flatbreads. Small individual breads were made daily.
- See also pages 2–4.

5 One of the more famous, if unfortunate, remarks attributed to Marie Antoinette was the notorious "Let them eat brioche (cake)." Cakes and tortes represent a high level of artistry and refinement of skill. Compare the quality of baked goods that are considered "homestyle" with those that are more often referred to as "pastries."

Homestyle	Pastries
Simple	Complex
Rustic	Refined
Basic doughs	Roll-ins, etc.
Little labor	Labor intensive
Less skill required	More difficult
Less ingredients	More ingredients
Less-expensive ingredients	More expensive

6 Discuss the benefits of offering cookies, candies, and confections to enhance the diner's meal.
- Lends a special touch to a guest's dining experience.
- Makes them feel like they got a gift—something free.
- Truffles, petits fours, simple candies can be a mark of distinction.
- See also pages 458–459.

Answer Key to Self-Study Questions

1 Preserve appropriate balance of ingredients to ensure that they have good rise, texture, consistency (crumb), color, and flavor.

2
- Chemical (baking soda and baking powder): alkali interacts with an acid to produce carbon dioxide which expands as it bakes
- Organic (yeast and sourdough): organisms that feed on sugars and give off carbon dioxide and alcohol

- Physical (steam): heated liquids in dough expand and cause item to rise as it bakes

3 Both contain proteins which provide stability. Proteins coagulate when exposed to heat, helping to provide structure.

4 Granules swell, trapping liquid or steam within its expanded framework (gelatinization).

5 Sugar attracts and holds moisture in baked goods; helps to extend shelf life.

6 It is a microscopic fungus which eats, breathes, grows, and reproduces.

7 Combine it with warm liquid and a small amount of flour (and some sugar, optional). Let it rest until a foam forms. If no foam forms, the yeast is dead and should not be used.

8 Purified animal protein used to stabilize or set. First bloomed in a cool liquid, then gently heated until dissolved, cooled, and added to a variety of items to enhance their stability.

9
- Aerates
- Removes lumps
- Filters impurities
- Evenly distributes dry ingredients

10
- To expel carbon dioxide
- To even out the overall temperature
- To redistribute the yeast evenly
- To introduce a fresh supply of oxygen to enable continued yeast activity

11 (a) Gluten is developed with proper kneading.
    (b) Provides the dough with the strength and elasticity to allow it to rise properly.

12
- Straight mixing method
- Creaming method
- Two-stage method
- Foaming method

13 (1) Dry ingredients are blended with all of the shortening and half of the liquid.
    (2) Combine eggs and other liquid ingredients, add in 2 or 3 stages and whip batter (3 minutes mixing time).
    (3) Mix an additional 3 minutes at higher speeds.
    (4) Scale into prepared pans and bake.

14 Vanilla sauce.

15 (1) Chop chocolate and place over a simmering water bath.

(2) Heat chocolate to a temperature of 105–110°F (40–43°C).

(3) Remove chocolate from the heat and stir until the temperature drops to between 87 and 92°F (30–33°C).

(4) Use chocolate immediately for dipping, coating, and decorating pastry items.

• Properly tempered chocolate sets quickly, has glossy (shiny) appearance, and good coating ability.

Keywords

Angel food cake: A type of sponge cake made with egg whites that are beaten until stiff.

Artisinal: Food producers practicing traditional methods for baking, cheesemaking, etc. Usually production is small and distribution is local.

Bake blind; baking blind: To partially or completely bake an unfilled pastry crust.

Basic pie dough *(pâte brisée):* A short dough made by combining flour, a fat, and water. Use to line pie and tart pans for sweet and savory tarts and pies.

Bavarian cream/Bavaroise: A type of custard made from heavy cream and eggs; it is sweetened, flavored, and stabilized with gelatin.

Blitz puff pastry: A dough similar to pie dough, but which contains a higher percentage of fat. It is rolled and folded in the same manner as traditional puff pastry.

Bloom: To soften gelatin in cool liquid before use.

Buttercream: A mixture of butter, sugar, and eggs or custard; it is used to garnish cakes and pastries.

Caramelization: The process of browning sugar in the presence of heat. The temperature range in which sugar caramelizes is approximately 320 to 360°F (160 to 182°C).

Chemical leavener: An ingredient or combination of ingredients (such as baking soda or baking powder) whose chemical action is used to produce carbon dioxide gas to leaven baked goods.

Chiffon cake: A cake made by the foaming method which contains a high percentage of eggs and sugar and relatively little if any fat.

Creaming method: A mixing method used for batters and doughs in which the fat and sugar are beaten together until light; dry and wet ingredients are added alternately to the batter.

Croissant dough: A dough consisting of a yeast dough with a butter roll-in, traditionally rolled in a crescent shape before baking.

Crumb: A term used to describe the texture of baked goods; for example, an item can be said to have a fine or coarse crumb.

Danish dough: A pastry dough consisting of rich yeast dough with a butter roll-in, possibly filled with nuts, fruit, or other ingredients and iced. This pastry originated in Denmark.

Dessert soufflé: A sweet egg-based dish, served as a dessert; made by combining a sweet base such as pastry cream or puréed fruits with beaten egg whites.

Dock; docked; docking: To cut the top of dough before baking to allow it to expand.

Foaming method: Cake batters made by first preparing a foam of eggs, egg whites, or egg yolks with sugar. Little if any fat is included in the batter.

Fondant: An icing made with sugar, water, and glucose; used primarily for pastry and confectionery.

Frozen desserts: Dishes served to conclude a meal that are churned (ice cream, sorbet) or still frozen (soufflé, granite, parfaits).

Fruit curd: Similar to a hollandaise sauce, made by cooking a fruit juice with sugar, eggs, and butter.

Ganache: A filling made of heavy cream, chocolate, and/or other flavorings.

Gelatin: A protein-based substance found in animal bones and connective tissue. When dissolved in hot liquid and then cooled, it can be used as a thickener and stabilizer.

Génoise (Fr.): A sponge cake made with whole eggs, used for petits fours, layer cakes, and other desserts.

Granita/granite: A still-frozen mixture of a flavored, sweetened liquid that is scraped just before service to produce flakes or crystals.

High-ratio cake: Made by preparing a batter that includes a high percentage of sugar in relation to other ingredients. Prepared by the two-stage mixing method.

Knead/kneading: The process of stretching dough repeatedly in order to give it a good consistency. Also helps to ensure proper quality in the finished baked item.

Lean dough: A yeast dough that includes very little or no fat.

Leavener: Any ingredient or process that produces air bubbles and causes the rising of baked goods. (See CHEMICAL, ORGANIC, PHYSICAL, and MECHANICAL LEAVENERS, YEAST, BAKING SODA, BAKING POWDER.)

Mousse (Fr.): A dish made with beaten egg whites and/or whipped cream folded into a flavored base appareil; may be sweet or savory.

Organic leavener: Yeast. A living organism. Operates by fermenting sugar to produce carbon dioxide gas, causing the batter to rise.

Parchment cones: Made from parchment paper, cut, rolled and folded to hold items that will be piped into designs.

Pastry cream: A thick sauce made by cooking together eggs, milk, sugar, and flavorings with a thickener; also known as creme patissière.

Pastry bag: A bag—usually made of plastic, canvas, or nylon—that can be fitted with plain or decorative tips and used to pipe out icings and puréed foods.

Pâte à choux (Fr.): Cream puff paste, made by boiling a mixture of water, butter, and flour, then beating in whole eggs.

Peel: A paddle used to transfer shaped doughs to a hearth or deck oven.

Phyllo dough: Pastry made with very thin sheets of a flour-and-water dough layered with butter and/or crumbs; similar to strudel. (Also called Filo.)

Physical leavener: Name given to the action of steam when trapped in a dough.

Proof: To allow yeast dough to rise. A proof box is a sealed cabinet that allows control over both temperature and humidity.

Puff pastry dough: A roll-in dough made by layering a lean, unleavened dough with butter, which is rolled and folded in the appropriate sequence.

Rich dough: A yeast dough that contains fats such as butter or egg yolks. May also contain sweeteners.

Roll-in (laminated) dough: Butter or a butter-based mixture that is placed between layers of pastry dough, then rolled and folded repeatedly to form numerous layers. When the dough is baked, the layers remain discrete, producing a very flaky, rich pastry.

Sabayon (Fr.): Wine custard. Sweetened egg yolks flavored with marsala or other wine or liqueur, beaten in a double boiler until frothy. (The Italian name is Zabaglione.)

Scale/scaling: To measure ingredients by weighing; to divide dough or batter into portions by weight.

Shorteners: Ingredients that have the effect of producing a small (or short) crumb in finished baked goods.

Sifting: Aerating flours, powders, starches, and other finely ground dry ingredients by passing them through a sieve or sifter.

Simple syrup: A mixture of water and sugar (with additional flavorings or aromatics as desired), heated until the sugar dissolves. Used to moisten cakes or to poach fruits.

Sourdough: Yeast dough leavened with a fermented starter instead of, or in addition to, fresh yeast. Some starters are kept alive by "feeding" with additional flour and water.

Sponge: A thick yeast batter that is allowed to ferment and develop a light, spongy consistency and is then combined with other ingredients to form a yeast dough.

Straight mixing method: The dough mixing method in which all ingredients are combined at once by hand or machine.

Strengtheners: Ingredients used in baking that give structure and stability to finished items (flour and eggs are two primary examples).

Sweeteners: Ingredients such as sugar, honey, or syrup; tend to aid flavor, moisture, and color to foods.

Temper: To heat gently and gradually. May refer to the process of incorporating hot liquid into a liaison to gradually raise its temperature. May also refer to the proper method for melting chocolate.

Thickeners: Ingredients used to give additional body to liquids; arrowroot, cornstarch, gelatin, roux, and beurre manié are examples.

Two-stage method: A procedure for preparing a batter for high-ratio cakes.

Vanilla sauce: Custard sauce made from milk or cream, sugar, and eggs.

Yeast: Microscopic fungus whose metabolic processes are responsible for fermentation. It is used for leavening bread and in cheese-, beer-, and winemaking.

Transparency Masters

Weights and Measures

Liquid Measures

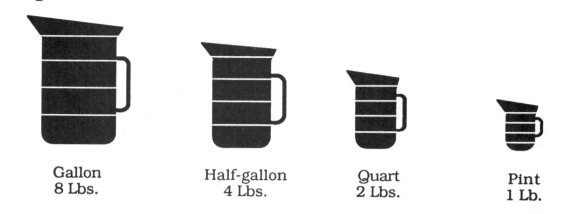

Gallon
8 Lbs.

Half-gallon
4 Lbs.

Quart
2 Lbs.

Pint
1 Lb.

Comparison

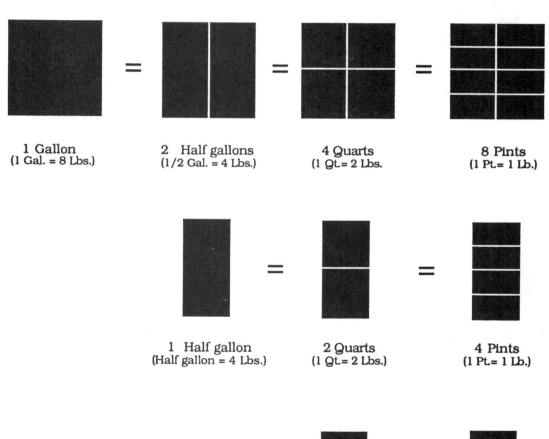

1 Gallon
(1 Gal. = 8 Lbs.)

2   Half gallons
(1/2 Gal. = 4 Lbs.)

4 Quarts
(1 Qt.= 2 Lbs.

8 Pints
(1 Pt.= 1 Lb.)

1   Half gallon
(Half gallon = 4 Lbs.)

2 Quarts
(1 Qt.= 2 Lbs.)

4 Pints
(1 Pt.= 1 Lb.)

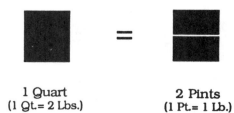

1 Quart
(1 Qt.= 2 Lbs.)

2 Pints
(1 Pt.= 1 Lb.)

Weights and Measures

 =  =  =

1 Gallon (128 oz.)	=	4 Quarts (1 Qt.=32 oz.)	=	8 Pints (1 Pt.=16 oz.)	=	16 Cups (1 cup=8oz.)

Gallon   Half-gallon   Quart   Pint

Can #	Fluid oz. Volume	Cups
6	4-3/4	1/2
303, also #1	15.6	2
303, cylinder	19.0	2-1/3
2	19.9	2-1/2
2, cylinder	23.0	3
2-1/2	28.5	3-1/2
#5 can	56.0	7
10	103.7	12-3/4
1 Gallon	128	16

Scoop Sizes	Measure/Tbsp.	Approximate Weight
# 40	1	3/4 to 1 oz.
30	2	1 to 1-1/2 oz.
24	2-2/3	1-1/2 to 1-3/4 oz.
20	3	1-3/4 to 2 oz.
16	4	2 to 2-1/2 oz.
12	5	2-1/2 to 3 oz.
10	6	4 to 5 oz.
6	10	6 oz.

Weights and Measures

Some common conversions

3 Teaspoons (tsp.)	. . . .	1 Tablespoon (Tbs.)
48 Teaspoons (tsp.)	. . . .	1 Cup (c.)
4 Tablespoons (Tbs.)	. . . .	1/4 Cup (c.)
16 Tablespoons (Tbs.)	. . . .	1 Cup (c.)
1/4 cup (c.)	. . . .	2 Ounces (oz.)
1/2 cup (c.)	. . . .	4 Ounces (oz.)
1 Gill	. . . .	4 Ounces (1/2 cup)

Metric Conversion Table

To Change	To	Multiply By
Ounces (oz.)	Grams (g)	28
Pounds (lbs.)	Kilograms (kg)	0.45
Fluid ounces (oz.)	Milleliters (ml)	30
Cups (c.)	Liters (l)	0.24
Pints (pt.)	Liters (l)	0.47
Quarts (qt.)	Liters (l)	0.95
Gallons (gal.)	Liters (l)	3.8
Temperature (F)	Temperature (C)	5/9 after subtracting 32

Platter Layout

Items

_____

_____

_____

_____

_____

_____

_____

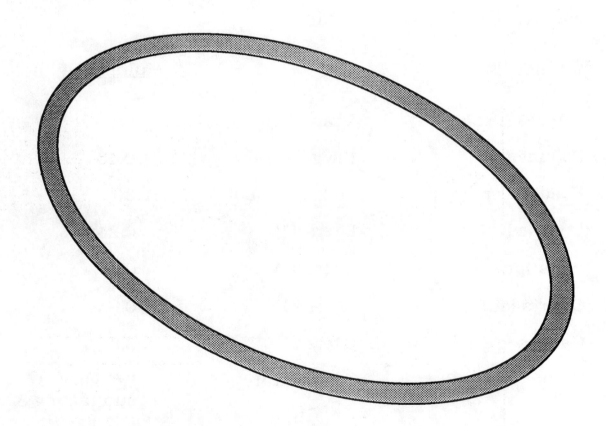

Plate Presentation

The Seven Nutritional Guidelines For Cooking

1. **MODERATE CALORIES.** Many Americans need to reduce their daily caloric intake in order to achieve a reasonable body weight (RBW). Excessive caloric intake has been linked to a variety of health risks because it leads to weight gain. Moderation of calories is the responsibility of the individual. However, the restaurant can help an individual achieve a RBW by providing healthy menu selections.

2. **MODERATE USE OF FAT-SPECIFICALLY SATURATED FAT-AND CONTROL DIETARY CHOLESTEROL.** Total fat use should not exceed 30% of total calories, saturated fat should not exceed 10% of total calories, and dietary cholesterol should be controlled to 300 milligrams or less, daily. This is the most important guideline to apply in the kitchen as well as one of the hardest to implement and still maintain high culinary standards.

3. **INCREASE USE OF COMPLEX CARBOHYDRATES, WHILE REDUCING USE OF SIMPLE SUGARS.** All carbohydrates used should comprise 50-60% or more of daily caloric intake. Complex carbohydrates which are high in vitamins, minerals and fiber should comprise 45-50% of total carbohydrates used, while simple carbohydrates, which provide little but calories, should be limited to 10% or less of total carbohydrates used.

4. **MODERATE USE OF PROTEIN.** Intake of protein should be approximately 15% of total calories. Excessive protein use is not necessary; protein foods tend to be higher in fat, saturated fat, and cholesterol.

5. **MODERATE USE OF SALT AND SODIUM.** Total daily sodium intake for most Americans should be reduced to less than 3,000 milligrams. When sodium is left out of a dish, the flavor may be adversely affected; the chef must focus on highlighting flavor by using other ingredients and methods.

6. **PROVIDE A WIDE VARIETY OF FOODS THAT ARE HIGH IN VITAMINS AND MINERALS (AND INCLUDE WATER AS A MAJOR BEVERAGE).** Many Americans consume too many refined and processed foods, which have a reduced nutritional value when compared to the fresh or whole foods. They also consume beverages which have limited nutrient content. It is important for the chef to purchase a variety of high quality, fresh products and to adhere to cooking and storing methods which preserve the product's nutrient content.

7. **SERVE ALCOHOL RESPONSIBLY, AND OFFER ALTERNATIVE BEVERAGES.** Alcohol contains a number of calories yet no known nutritional value. Excessive alcohol is also known to deplete the body of essential vitamins and minerals. It is the responsibility of the restaurant to provide wines by the glass and low-alcohol and non-alcohol beverage alternatives.

Making the necessary changes to initiate these guidelines in the kitchen and restaurant takes time. It is necessary for the chef and restaurateur to gradually implement these seven nutritional guidelines. (Begin with a small menu section of healthy food choices in order to allow for the time necessary to train staff members and to receive customer feedback. As both the staff and the customer become more familiar with the new menu concept, expansion can occur and be endorsed by all.)

KNIFE CUTS
(SHOWN ACTUAL SIZE)

It should be noted that these dimensions are recommended guidelines and are used here at The Culinary Institute of America to stress consistency and develop discipline for your knife skills. In common practice (outside the Institute) professional chefs may not measure exactly to these guidelines. However, in most circumstances consistency will be expected.

JULIENNE
1/16 x 1/16 x 1"-2"

*ALLUMETTE
1/8 x 1/8 x 1"-2"
*This cut technically refers only to the cutting of potatoes 1/4"x 1/4" x 2"

BATONNET
1/4 x 1/4 x 2"-2 1/2"

BRUNOISE
1/8 x 1/8 x 1/8"

SMALL DICE
1/4 x 1/4 x 1/4"

MEDIUM DICE
1/3 x 1/3 x 1/3"

LARGE DICE
3/4 x 3/4 x 3/4"

PAYSANNE
1/2 x 1/2 x 1/8"

TORNEE
2 " x 7 SIDES

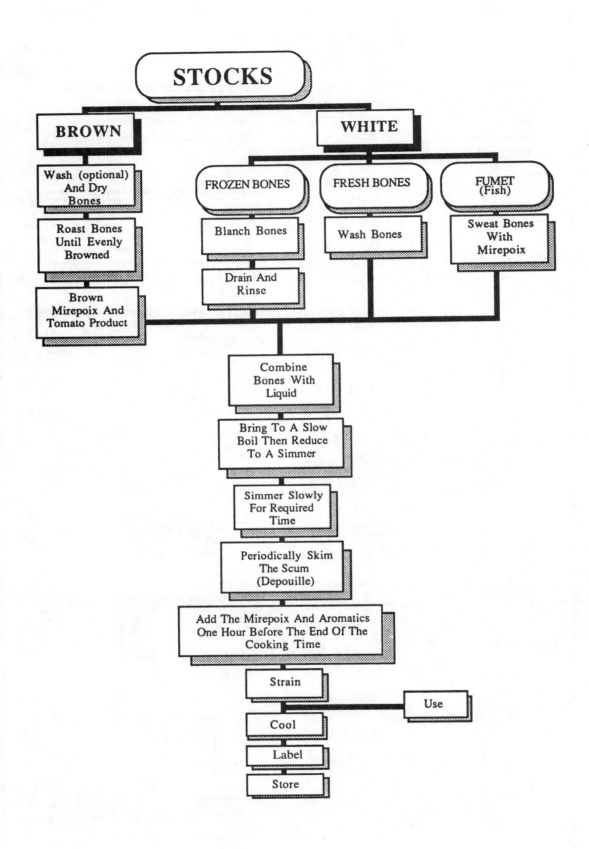

STOCKS

BROWN

- Wash (optional) And Dry Bones
- Roast Bones Until Evenly Browned
- Brown Mirepoix And Tomato Product

WHITE

FROZEN BONES
- Blanch Bones
- Drain And Rinse

FRESH BONES
- Wash Bones

FUMET (Fish)
- Sweat Bones With Mirepoix

- Combine Bones With Liquid
- Bring To A Slow Boil Then Reduce To A Simmer
- Simmer Slowly For Required Time
- Periodically Skim The Scum (Depouille)
- Add The Mirepoix And Aromatics One Hour Before The End Of The Cooking Time
- Strain
- Cool
- Label
- Store

- Use

CONVECTION SIMMERING

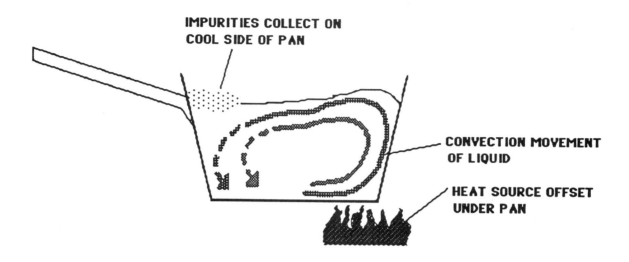

IMPURITIES COLLECT ON
COOL SIDE OF PAN

CONVECTION MOVEMENT
OF LIQUID

HEAT SOURCE OFFSET
UNDER PAN

Cooling Stocks

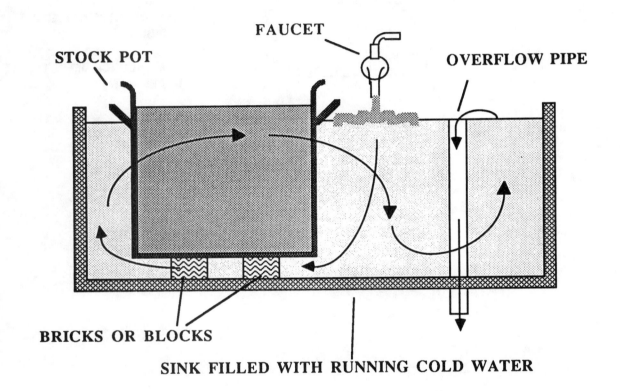

FAUCET

STOCK POT

OVERFLOW PIPE

BRICKS OR BLOCKS

SINK FILLED WITH RUNNING COLD WATER

The Stages of Consommé during Clarification

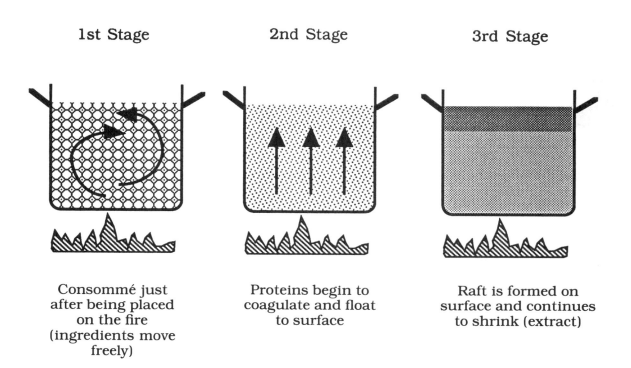

1st Stage

2nd Stage

3rd Stage

Consommé just after being placed on the fire (ingredients move freely)

Proteins begin to coagulate and float to surface

Raft is formed on surface and continues to shrink (extract)

How to Incorporate Roux

Adding stock to roux

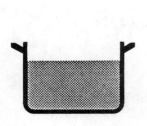

1.

Hot stock

2.

Add stock to roux 1/3
at a time, whisking
with each addition

3.

Whisk until liquid
comes to a simmer

Adding roux to stock

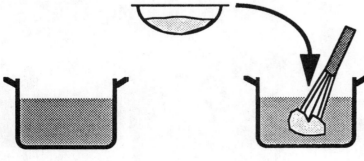

1.

Hot stock

2.

Add roux to stock,
whisking until roux is
dissolved

3.

Whisk until liquid
comes to a simmer

Note: The best results are achieved when stock and roux are opposite temperatures.

How to Incorporate Roux

Tempering or slurry method

1. Cold stock

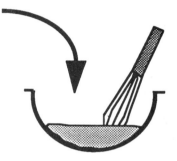

2. Add 1/4 of the stock to the roux, mix well

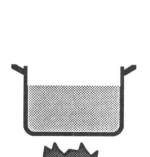

3. Heat the stock to just under the boiling point

4. Add roux stock mixture, whisking until totally incorporated

5. Whisk until liquid comes to a simmer

Broilers and Grills

Broiler

Heat source radiates heat
from above
Limited conduction from
the heat of the grids

Types of broilers:

Conventional gas or electric
Convection gas or electric

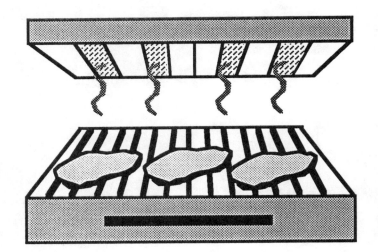

Grill

Heat source radiates
from below
Conduction and radiation
of heat

Types of grills:

Gas, Charcoal,
Hardwood

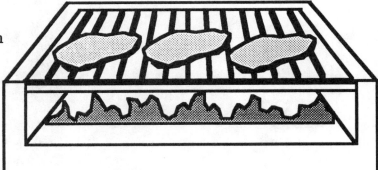

Marination

Marinade: A savory, usually acidic liquid in which meat, fish, or a vegetable is soaked to enrich its flavor or to tenderize it.

Why?

Preservation: Historically

Flavor: Primary Reason

Tenderize: Secondary Reason

Components:

Acid: To tenderize, preserve, and flavor
(Vinegar, citrus juices, wines)

Aromatics: To flavor (Herbs and spices)

Oil: To protect, preserve and flavor

Salt: To preserve and flavor

Vegetables: To flavor

How to Mark a Steak

Place steak on grids of preheated broiler or grill

Cook until grill marks are well defined

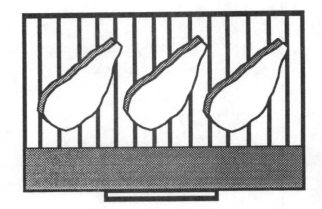

Turn steaks at a 45° angle

Cook until grill marks are well defined

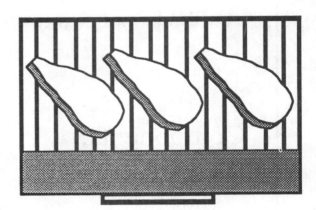

Turn steaks over

Continue to cook to customer's specifications

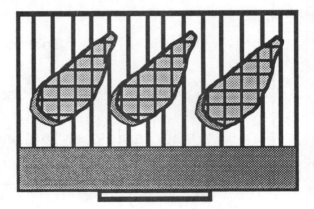

Broil, Grill B.B.Q. of Red Meats	Chopped Steak	Thin Steaks	Medium Steaks	Thick Steaks	Thin Lamb Chops	Variety Meats Kidneys, Livers	Thick Lamb Chops
Season	--	X	X	X	X	--	X
Marinade	--	X	X	X	X	X	X
High heat	X	X	X	X	X	X	X
High heat & Reduce	X	--	X	X	X	X	X
High heat & finish in oven	--	--	--	X	--	--	X
Carry-over cooking	--	--	--	X	--	--	X

Techniques for Broiled Fish

	Skinless Fillets	Skin on Fillets	Whole Fish	Steaks	Lobster	Scallops Shrimp, en brochette	
Plain } Drizzled with fat	X	X	X	X	X	X	
Flour } Drizzled with fat	X	X	X	X	--	--	
Crumbs } Drizzled with fat	X	X	X	X	X	X	
Season	X	X	X	X	--	X	
Marinade	X	X	X	X	--	X	
High heat	X	X	X	X	X	X	
High heat & reduce	X	X	X	X	X	X	
High heat & oven	X	X	X	X	X	X	
Moderate heat	X	X	X	X	--	--	
Baste	X	X	X	X	X	X	
Hand grill	X	X	X	X	X	--	
Scored	--	X	X	--	--	--	

Basting with a brush is beneficial to the item being broiled.

A common practice of cooking fish on a sizzler platter under the broiler
and finish in the oven is often referred to as being broiled. It is not
a true broil. It is actually baking the fish.

Broiled White Meats	Veal	Pork	Chicken	Variety Meats	Small Game Birds
Season	X	X	X	--	X
Marinade	X	X	X	X	X
High heat & reduced	X	X	X	X	X
Moderate heat	X	X	X	X	X
Baste	X	X	X	X	X
Carry - over cooking	X	X	X	X	X
Hand grill	--	--	X	--	X

Roasting

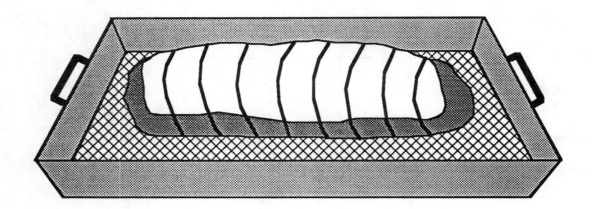

In Roasting the following are required:

Open, low-sided pan

Seasoned meat, barded and tied

Rack used to hold meat above the bottom of the pan

Roasting	(Standard Ratio)	
Ingredients:		
1	#	Meat (prepared as desired)
1	oz.	Mirepoix (cut according to cooking time)
2	oz.	Finished sauce per portion

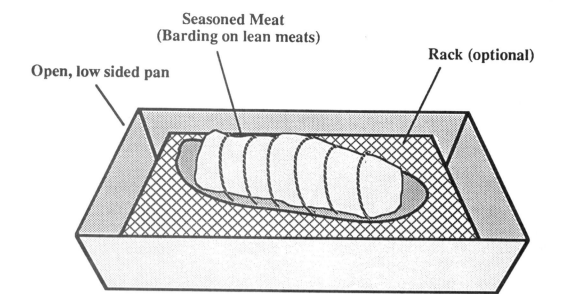

Open, low sided pan   Seasoned Meat
(Barding on lean meats)   Rack (optional)

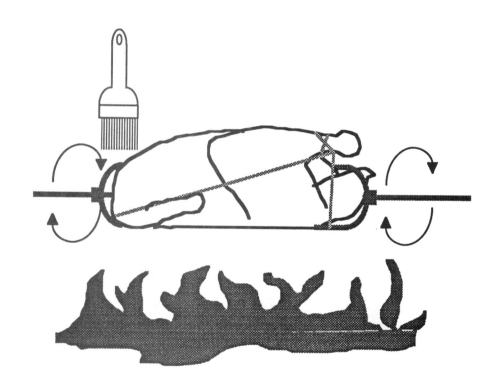

Degrees of Doneness for Meats and Poultry

Item	Desired Degree of Doneness	Temperature at which to remove item from oven
Red Meats		
	Rare	125° F
	Medium	135° F
	Well done	145° F
Pork	Well done	165°F
Veal	Medium well	140°F
Poultry	Well done	160°F (thigh)
Fish	Well done	140°F

Carry-Over Cooking

The amount of time a product continues to cook once it is removed from the heat source. Carry-over cooking affects all foods, the larger the item the longer the carry-over.

Testing Roasted Items for Doneness

Item	What to Check	Pro/Con
Fork (2-Tined)	Color of juices in poultry	Punctures meat, loss of juices
Skewer	Resistance and temperature with other meats	Not accurate
Bi-Therm Thermometer	Temperature of desired doneness	Inexpensive. accurate The best and most consistent method
Time/Temperature to Weight Ratio	Follow chart to determine how long at what temperature	Inaccurate, the shape of the meat will affect the cooking time Good for an estimate on approximate cooking time
Touch	Resistance of fibers in the meat As the meat cooks the fibers tighten	Inaccurate, resistance varies with the age and type of meat
Experience	All of the above	Helps to control variables

Temperatures for Roasting Meats

Temperature	Items cooked by this method	Comments
HIGH HEAT **375 - 475° F**	Feathered game Domestic poultry Water fowl Smaller cuts of red meat	Excessive caramelization, shrinkage and drying Renders fat and crisps skin in water fowl Good for small cuts that cook quickly
MODERATE HEAT **325 - 350° F**	All meats, poultry and game	Good caramelization, less shrinkage and crusting than high heat
LOW HEAT **275 - 300°F**	Red meats Feathered game Domestic poultry Water fowl	Better yields on larger cuts Good for conventional ovens
CONTROLLED HEAT **200° F**	Larger cuts of red meat White meat Domestic poultry	Best method for high yields Jus or drippings not obtainable at this low temperature Very little caramelization

Larding and Barding

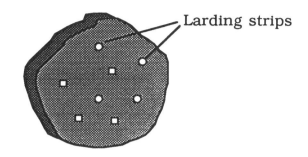

Larding strips

Cross section of
larded meat

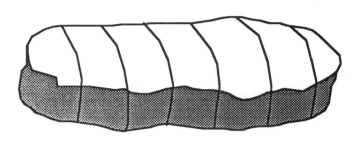

Barded meat ready for
roasting

Larding - Inserting strips of fat into meat with the use of a special needle. Pork back fat is commonly used as it is easy to handle. The fat adds moisture to the meat.

Barding - Covering meat with a thin layer of fat. This technique is used on meats that do not have a natural fat layer. The fat melts during roasting and prevents the meat from drying out.

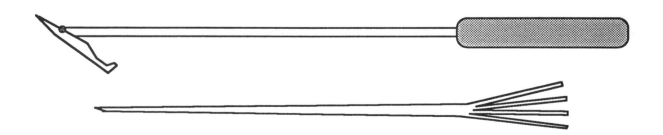

Larding Needles

TECHNIQUE OF ROASTING	FURRED GAME	FEATHERED GAME	DOMESTIC DUCK/ GEESE	POULTRY/ CHICKEN/ TURKEY/ CAPON	WATER FOWL	WHITE MEATS/ VEAL/ PORK	COMMENTS
SEASONING	X	X	X	X	X	X	
PLACED ON RACK	X	X	X	X	NO	X	
SEARING 400 F. 450 F.	X	X	X	X	X	X	
HIGH HEAT 475 F.	NO	X	X	X	X	NO	
MODERATE 325 F 350 F	X	X	X	X	X	X	
LOW 275 F. 300 F.	NO	X	X	X	X	X	
CONTROLLED 200 F.	NO	NO	NO	X	NO	X	JUS IS NOT OBTAINABLE IN THIS TEMPERATURE RANGE.
MIREPOIX	X	X	X	X	X	X	
JUS	** X	** X	X	X	** X	X	
RESTING PERIOD	X	X	X	X	X	X	
CARRY-OVER COOKING	X	X	X	X	X	X	
LARDED	X	X	X	X	X	X	
BARDED	X	X	X	X	X	X	

** IN SOME INSTANCES DEMI-GLACE IS USED AS A BASE FOR SAUCE.

Sauté

Sauté is a French verb meaning " to leap or jump". This translation, however, has little to do with the sauteing of most meat and seafood items. Because it does not translate easily into English, the word has become part of our culinary vocabulary just as other French words (maitre d´hotel, garde manger) have.

Pans used for Sauté

A shallow pan is used for sauté because it allows moisture to escape (if moisture is trapped in the pan it causes the food to steam, there will be no browning and meat will become tough).

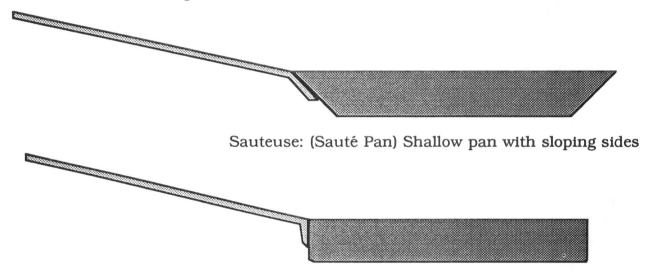

Sauteuse: (Sauté Pan) Shallow pan with **sloping sides**

Sautoir: Shallow pan with **straight sides**

In Sautéing the following are required:

A hot pan with a small amount of fat

Thin tender food items with excess moisture blotted off

Correct size pan for the amount of food to be cooked

All mise en place required for preparing the item

Sauté

Traditionally, sautéing is done on top of the stove, but may be finished in a moderate oven.

Sautéed items are cooked to order.

The main characteristic of this cooking method is that it is a dry procedure,(the absence of moisture/liquid), uses only fat (i.e. butter or oil) and the process of deglazing is necessary for all sautes in the classical standard.

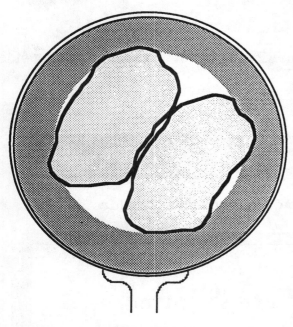

Incorrect

The pan is overcrowded, trapping steam which will prevent the meat from browning and cause the meat fibers to toughen .

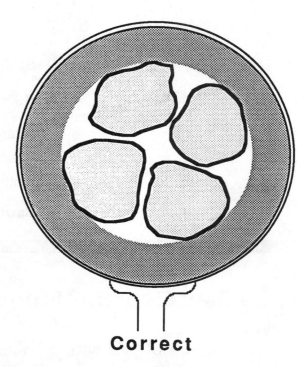

Correct

The pan is full but there is sufficient space between the pieces of meat, allowing steam to escape and prevent toughening.

Pan-Frying

Pan-frying and saute are similar techniques in that the foods are cooked in fat in shallow, wide pans. From then on the techniques differ:

Cross section of items cooking by Pan-Frying

* Food is thicker than sauteed food
* More fat is used
* Lower heat and longer cooking time
* Food is coated
* A sauce is not derived by deglazing the pan

Cross section of items cooking by Sauté

* Items are thinner than pan-fried food
* Very little fat is used
* Higher heat and quicker cooking time
* Items are not usually coated
* A sauce is derived from deglazing the pan

In Pan-Frying the following are required:

A hot pan with the correct amount of fat

Thin, tender food items, dredged in flour or coated

Absorbent paper to drain finished products on

A pre-prepared sauce derived from a different source

Saute of Red Meat	Thin Pieces up to 1" Thick	Thick Pieces Over 1" Thick	Emince	Livers	Kidneys
Meat Should Be Dry	X	X	X	X	X
Season	X	X	X	X	X
Nature	X	X	X	X and flour	X
Small Amount of Fat	X	X	X	X	X
Brisk Moderate Heat	X	X	NO	X	NO
High Heat	X	NO	X	X	X
Cooked Entirely On Range	X	X	X	X	X
Started on Range And Finished In Oven	NO	X	NO	NO	NO
Garnish Cooked Separately	X	X	X	X	X
Deglazed	X	X	X	X	X
Sauce Made In Same Pan	X	X	X	X	X
Reheat Gently In Finished Sauce	X	NO	X	X	X

APPROXIMATE GUIDELINES

DESCRIPTION	Weight Per Each	Thickness
Filet Mignon	5 oz.	1 "
Filet Steak	7 oz.	1 1/2 "
Tournedos	3 - 4 oz.	1 "
Single Chateaubriand	11 oz.	3 "
Entrecote	7 oz.	1/2 "

Saute of White Meat	Emince	Cutlets	Chops	Medallions	Kidneys
Meat Should Be Dry	X	X	X	X	X
Season	X	X	X	X	X
Nature	X	X	X	X	X
Flour	X	X	X	X	NO
Smalll Amount Of Fat	X	X	X	X	X
Brisk Medium Heat	NO	X	X	X	NO
High Heat and Then lowered	X	X	X	X	X
Uncovered	X	X	X	X	X
Cooked Entirely On Range	X	X	X	X	X
Started On Range And Finished In Oven	X	NO	X	NO	NO
Garnish Cooked Separately	X	X	X	X	X
Deglazing	X	X	X	X	X
Sauce Made In Same Pan	X	X	X	X	X
Reheat Gently In Finished Sauce	X	X	X	X	X

Saute of Poultry	Supreme	Disjointed	Dishes of Saute	Feathered Game	Specialty (Livers)
Product Should Be Dry	X	X	X	X	X
Seasoned	X	X	X	X	X
Nature	X	X	X	X	X
Flour	X	X	X	X	X
Small Amount of Fat	X	X	X	X	X
Moderate Amount of Fat	X	X	X	X	X
Brisk Medium Heat	X	X	X	X	X
High Heat	X	X	X	X	X
Uncovered	X	X	X	X	X
Covered	X	X	X	X	NO
Cooked Entirely On The Range	X	NO	NO	X	X
Started On Range Finished In Oven	X	X	X	X	NO
Deglazing	X	X	X	X	X
Sauce Made in Same Pan	X	X	X	X	X
Reheat Gently In Finished Sauce	X	X	NO	X	X

** Note that feathered game (except breast of pheasant) are generally cooked rare and with high heat.

There are two approaches to preparation in saute of poultry:

1) A blanc (white) where the preparation involves firming the meat without browning and the sauce is generally finished with cream.

2) A brun (brown) where the poultry is seared and a brown color is desired.

Saute Of Fish	Fillets	Small Whole Fish	Specialty Roe-Milk	Steaks	Crustacean Lobster, Soft Shell Crab, Shrimp
Marinate	X	X	X	X	X
Product Should Be Dry	X	X	X	X	X
Season	X	X	X	X	X
Nature	X	X	X	X	X
Flour	X	X	X	X	X
Small Amount of Fat	X	X	X	X	X
Moderate Amount of Fat	X	X	X	X	X
Low Heat	NO	NO	X	X	NO
Brisk Medium Heat	X	X	X	X	X
High Heat	X	NO	NO	NO	X
Uncovered	X	X	X	X	X
Covered	NO	NO	X	NO	NO
Cooked Entirely On Range	X	X	X	X	X
Started On Range Finished In Oven		X	X	X	X
Garnish Cooked Separately	X	X	X	X	X
Sauce Made In Same Pan	X	NO	NO	X	X

Doré (translation: golden brown)

Fish that has been sauteed until golden brown and served plain.
No sauce.

a la Meuniere (translation: In the style of the miller's wife)

Fish that has been dredged in flour, sauteed to a golden brown and finished with lemon juice, chopped parsley and brown butter.

Deep-Fat Frying

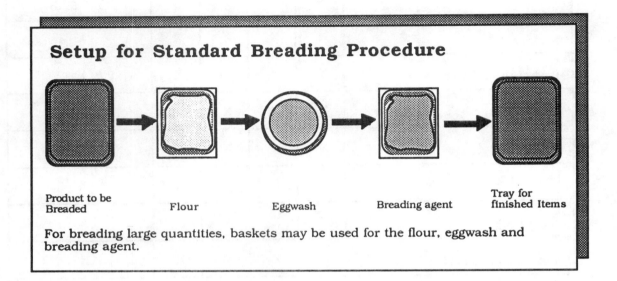

Setup for Standard Breading Procedure

Product to be Breaded	Flour	Eggwash	Breading agent	Tray for finished Items

For breading large quantities, baskets may be used for the flour, eggwash and breading agent.

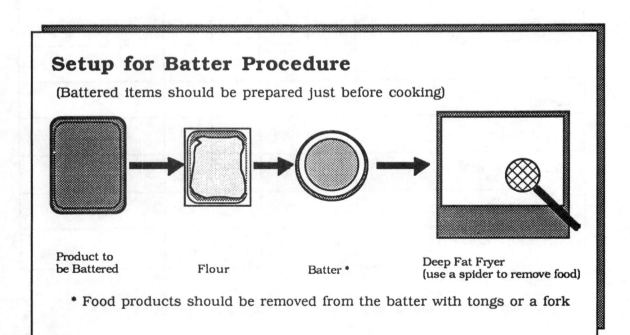

Setup for Batter Procedure

(Battered items should be prepared just before cooking)

Product to be Battered	Flour	Batter *	Deep Fat Fryer (use a spider to remove food)

* Food products should be removed from the batter with tongs or a fork

Deep-Fat Frying

Care of the frying fat:

Skim fat frequently

Maintain proper operating temperature between 250 - 375° F.

Turn down fryer when not in use

Strain fat daily, more often if necessary

Add new fat as necessary

Change fat when required

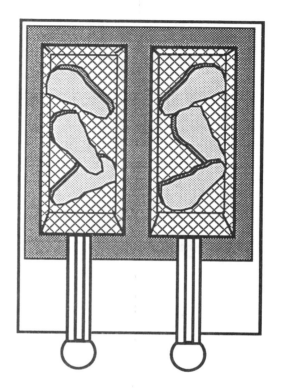

In Deep-Fat Frying the following are required:

Clean fat

Fat preheated to the proper temperature

Proper mise en place for the item to be fried

Tray with absorbent paper to drain finished food

Deep-Fat Frying

Basket Method vs. Swimming Method

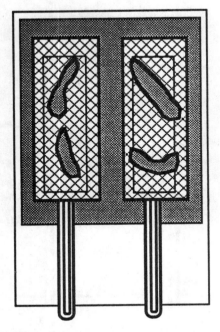

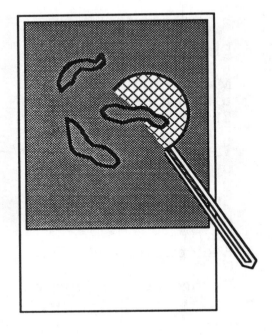

Basket Method: requires placing the food in the fryer baskets, then immersing the baskets in hot fat.

Swimming Method: requires the product to be placed directly into the hot fat. The food will be agitated and removed with a spider.

Deep-Fat Frying Methods:

Item	Basket Method	Swimming Method
Breaded or other dry coating	Yes	Optional (Basket is preferred)
Many small pieces	Yes	No
Battered items	No	Yes
Large items	Yes (if they fit)	Yes

DEEP - FAT FRYING	Fish	Uncooked Meats	Cooked Meats (Croquettes)	Vegetables	Cheese	Savouries Fritters	Pate au choux	Potatoes	Vegetable or Starch Croquettes	Fruit
Plain	--	--	--	--	--	--	X	X	X	--
Francaise	X	X	X	X	--	--	--	--	X	--
Anglaise	X	X	X	X	X	X	--	X	X	X
Dough Wrapped	X	X	X	X	X	X	--	--	--	X
Batter	X	X	X	X	X	X	--	--	X	X
Special (Coconut) (Villeroy)	X	X	X	X	X	X	--	--	--	--
250 - 270 deg.F. Blanch	--	--	--	--	--	--	--	X	--	--
300 - 350 deg.F. Moderate Heat	X	X	X	X	--	--	X	X	X	--
350 - 375 deg.F. Hot Heat	X	X	X	X	X	X	X	X	X	X
375 - 400 deg.F. Very Hot Heat	X	X	X	X	X	X	--	X	X	X

Enemies of Frying Fat

High temperatures
Free fatty acids (bacon fat, etc.)
Moisture
Exposure to air
Certain metals (i.e., aluminum)
Salt
Food particles

Indications that Frying Fat Needs Changing

Low smoking point
Foaming
Color
Product absorbs excessive fat
Product darkens too quickly
Product cooks too slowly
Resin forms on top
Flavor or product changes
Unpleasant odor

Boiling (212° F +)

Visually what water will look like at the following temperatures:

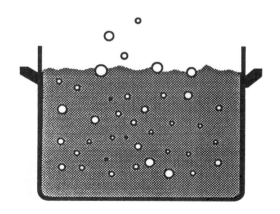

210° F   Very rapid release of large bubbles; beginning of a rolling agitation

212° F   Rapid rolling boil

212° F + Adding salt to the water will increase the temperature at which the water boils

The pot used for boiling should have a large surface area

In boiling the following are required:

Large pot, plenty of water

Food item (vegetables and pasta are the most common foods boiled)

Salt in the water (optional)

Water maintained at a rolling boil during cooking

Cold water if shocking is required after boiling

Simmering   (185 - 205° F)

Visually what water will look like at
the following temperatures:

190° F   Increase of large bubble
quantity with condensed
packages of bubbles

195° F   Minimal agitation caused by
bubbles

200° F   Very rapid dispersion of
bubbles; agitation around sides
of pot.

205° F   Surface agitation, mostly on
sides with very rapid release
of bubbles of large size and
quantity.

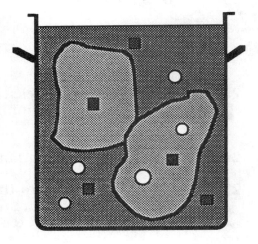

**A pot that is taller
than it is wide is used
to simmer various
meats. The shape of
the pot prevents
excess evaporation.**

In simmering the following are required:

Tall, narrow pot

Tougher, more mature cut of meat or poultry

Product started in cold liquid

Liquid maintained at a gentle simmer during cooking

Shallow-Poaching

(140 - 185° F)

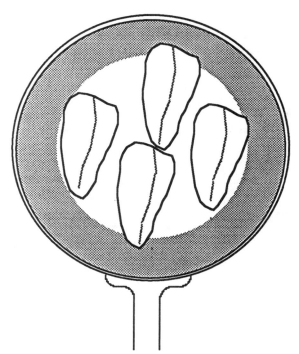

Visually what water will look like
at the following temperatures:

140° F   Minute bubbles adhere to
sides and bottom of pan.

150° F   Same as above with
increase of bubble quantity.

160° F   Bubbles begin to increase in
size.

180° F   Increased size of bubble
with large quantity of
bubbles coming to surface.

Diagram showing the
correct spacing for
shallow poached fish

In shallow poaching the following are required:

Shallow wide pan

Tender portion-size items

Liquid maintained at a very slow simmer during cooking

Sauce is made from the poaching liquid

Shallow vs. Submerge-Poaching

Cross section view of poaching techniques

Shallow-Poach   Submerge-Poach

The differences in poaching techniques:

Shallow	Submerge
Less liquid is used	More liquid is used
Smaller cuts of poultry, meat or fish	Larger cuts can be poached by this method
A sauce is made from the poaching liquid	The poaching liquid is not used for the sauce, a separately derived sauce is used
Poaching generally is done in the oven	Cooking is done on top of the stove
The garnish may be included during the cooking	The garnish is cooked separately and added just before serving
The pan is covered with a paper cover	The pan is not covered

POACHING OF FISH		Large Whole Fish	Small Whole Fish	Fillets	Steaks	Crustaceans	Mollusks
Fish Stock		--	X	X	X	--	--
Red Wine		X	X	X	X	--	--
White Wine	COURT BOULLION	X	X	X	X	X	X
Plain (Water, Milk, Lemon)		X	X	X	X	--	--
Salted Water		X	X	X	X	X	--
Vinegar or Lemon		X	X	X	X	X	--
Cooked in the Oven		X	X	X	X	--	--
Cooked on Top of The Stove		X	X	X	X	X	X
Reduced Cooking Liquid is used as part of the Sauce		X	X	X	X	--	X
Separate Sauce is made NOT using Cooking Liquid		X	X	X	X	--	X
Individual Portions (a la carte) Small Amount of Liquid		--	--	X	X	X	X
Large Amount of Liquid		X	X	X	X	X	X

Poaching Temperature Range: 140F. to 185F.

Poaching, Simmering and Boiling

Poaching, simmering and boiling all cook foods in the same way, i.e. in liquid, and are therefore known as moist-heat methods. The liquid may be water or a stock or sauce. It is the temperature of the liquid that marks the difference between the three methods:

$$140 \text{ to } 185 \text{ deg.F. -- Poaching}$$
$$190 \text{ to } 205 \text{ deg.F. -- Simmering}$$
$$212 \text{ deg.F. } + \quad \text{ -- Boiling}$$

Visually, the progression in raising the temperature of 2 quarts of water (with and without salt) are clearly seen:

	2 quarts water	2 quarts of water +salt (salt usage 1 to 4 1/2 tbs.)
140 deg.F.	Minute bubbles adhere to sides and bottom of pan.	Cloudiness occurred with use of 3 tbs. or more of salt.
150 deg.F.	Same as above with increase of bubble quantity.	The use of salt between 140 deg.F. and 185 deg.F. eliminated the small or minute bubbles.
160 deg.F.	Minute bubbles begin to break from bottom.	
170 deg.F.	Bubbles begin to increase in size.	
180 deg.F.	Increased size of bubble with large quantity of bubbles coming to surface.	
190 deg.F.	Increase of large bubble quantity with condensed packages of bubbles	Large bubbles coming to surface with increase in bubble quantity.
195 deg.F.	Minimal agitation caused by bubbles	Large bubbles forming on bottom and breaking, like flashes.
200 deg.F.	Very rapid dispersion of bubbles; agitation round sides.	Release of steam; water appears to roll.
205 deg.F.	Surface agitation, mostly on sides with very rapid release of bubbles of large size and quantity.	Movement on sides; large bubble with small bubbles on bottom surfacing with agitation.
210 deg.F.	Very rapid release of large bubbles; beginning of a rolling agitation.	Increase of large bubbles beginning to roll gently.
212 deg.F.	Rapid rolling boil	Gently rolling boil.
213 deg.F. 215 deg.F.		High rapid boil using 3 to 4 1/2 tbs. salt per 2 quarts of water.

POACHING OF FISH		Large Whole Fish	Small Whole Fish	Fillets	Steaks	Crustaceans	Mollusks
Fish Stock		--	X	X	X	--	--
Red Wine		X	X	X	X	--	--
White Wine	COURT BOUILLON	X	X	X	X	X	X
Plain (Water, Milk, Lemon)		X	X	X	X	--	--
Salted Water		X	X	X	X	X	--
Vinegar or Lemon		X	X	X	X	X	--
Cooked in the Oven		X	X	X	X	--	--
Cooked on Top of The Stove		X	X	X	X	X	X
Reduced Cooking Liquid is used as part of the Sauce		X	X	X	X	--	X
Separate Sauce is made NOT using Cooking Liquid		X	X	X	X	--	X
Individual Portions (a la carte) Small Amount of Liquid		--	--	X	X	X	X
Large Amount of Liquid		X	X	X	X	X	X

Poaching Temperature Range: 140F. to 185F.

Braising

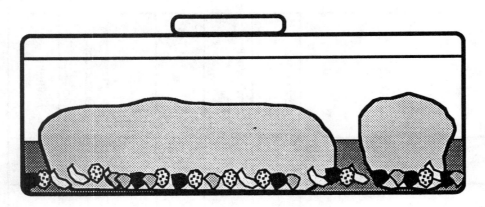

In Braising the following are required:

Brazier with tightfitting lid

Prepared meat (larded, tied, seasoned or marinated)

Correct size pan for the amount of meat to be braised

Correct amount of liquid

Braising		(Standard Ratio)
Ingredients:		
1	#	Meat
1	oz.	Mirepoix
1	pint	Liquid (stock, sauce or other)
	The ratio of liquid for braising is 3 - 5 oz. per portion	

BRAISING

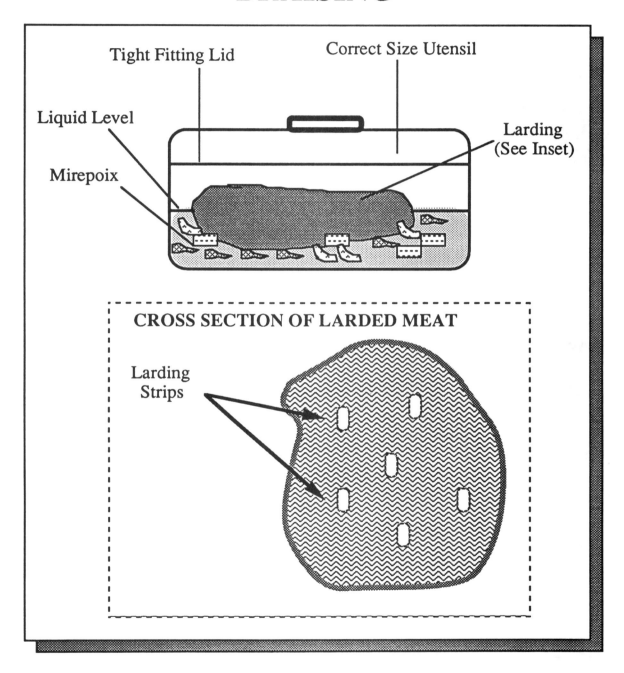

Tight Fitting Lid

Correct Size Utensil

Liquid Level

Mirepoix

Larding
(See Inset)

CROSS SECTION OF LARDED MEAT

Larding
Strips

Braising vs. Stewing

Braising   Stewing

Relationship of meat to amount of sauce

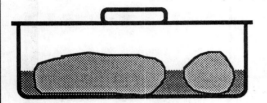 

The lid is optional if
cooking is done on top
of the stove

Braising		Stewing
Large, multi-portion	**Size of meat**	Small pieces
Covers 1/2-1/3 of meat	**Amount of liquid**	Covers meat
Cooked separately	**Garnish**	Cooked with meat or separately
Strained	**Sauce**	Not strained
In oven	**Cooking**	In oven or on top of the range

Stewing: Is a variation of the braising method

THE SAUSAGE PRESS (STUFFER)

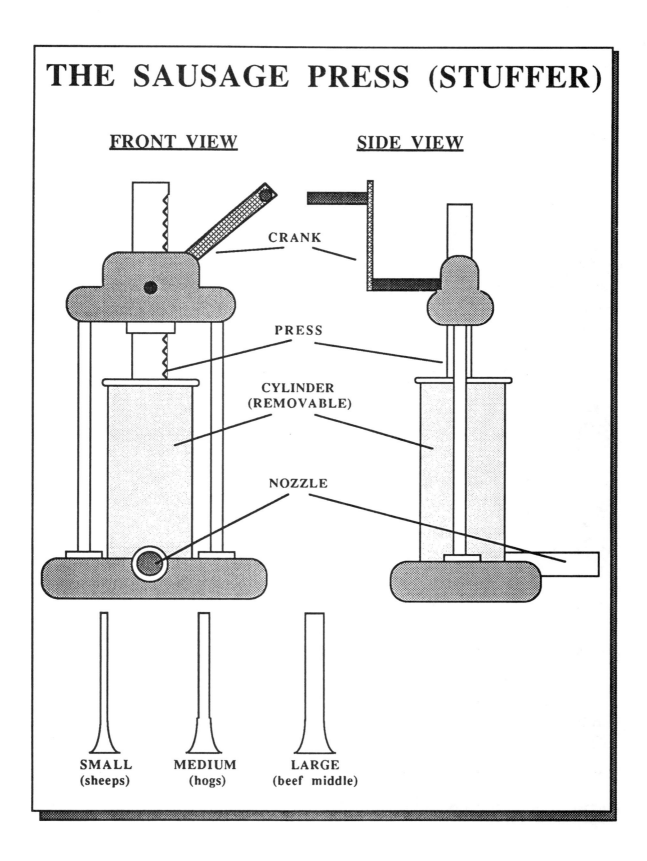

FRONT VIEW

SIDE VIEW

CRANK

PRESS

CYLINDER
(REMOVABLE)

NOZZLE

SMALL
(sheeps)

MEDIUM
(hogs)

LARGE
(beef middle)

Assembly of the Grinder Head

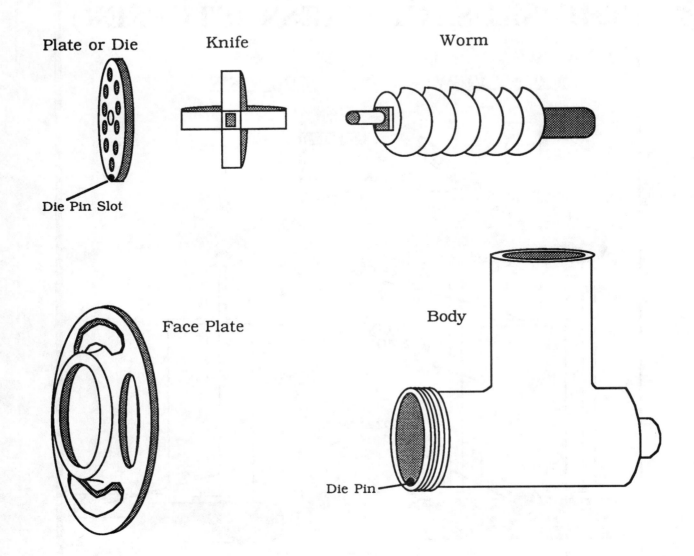

Plate or Die

Die Pin Slot

Knife

Worm

Face Plate

Body

Die Pin

1. Attach body to drive unit (mixer) and tighten thumbscrew on drive unit.

2. Insert worm into grinder body.

3. Slip knife onto worm shaft making sure that the flat side of blade is facing out.

4. Slip die onto worm shaft and lock die pin slot into die pin inside body.

5. Turn faceplate onto body, making sure that die pin and slot are locked together.

Basic Ratios

Ingredients	Custard	Vanilla sauce	Pastry cream	Bavarian cream	Whipped cream	Ice cream	Mousse	Parfait	Meringue	German butter cream	French butter cream	Swiss butter cream	Italian butter cream
Milk	1 qt.	1 qt.	1 qt.	1 qt.		1/2 qt.				X			
Heavy Cream				1 qt.	1 qt.	1/2 qt.	1 qt.	1 qt.					
Sugar	8 oz.	8 oz.	8 oz.	8 oz.	1-2 oz.	8 oz.	8 oz.	16 oz.	3-5 lb.	X	X	X	X
Eggs (each)	6-8		6-8	6-8						X			
Egg Yolks (each)		12-16				6-8	8	20			X		
Egg Whites (each)							8		1 qt.				X
Starch			2-3 oz.							X			
Butter			2-4 oz.							X	X	X	X
Gelatin				1 oz.									
Water				8 oz.								X	
Flavorings	X	X	X	X	X	X	X	X	X	X	X	X	X

Basic Dough Ratios

Basic Bread Dough	Hard Roll Dough	Soft roll Dough	Croissant Dough	Danish Dough	Puff-paste Dough
1 qt. Water	1 qt. Water	1 qt. Water	1 qt. Milk	1 qt. Milk	1 qt. Water
2 oz. Yeast	2 oz. Yeast	3 oz. Yeast	3 oz. Yeast	8 oz. Yeast	
1 oz. Salt	1-1/4 oz. Salt	1-1/4 oz. Salt	1-1/4 oz. Salt	1-1/2 oz. Salt	1 oz. Salt
1 oz. Sugar	1-1/4 oz. Sugar	5 oz. Sugar	3 oz. Sugar	10 oz. Sugar	
4 lb. Flour	3 lb. 12 oz. Flour	3 lb. 10 oz. Flour	3 lb. 10 oz. Flour	4 lb. 10 oz. Flour	4 lb. Flour
Butter			2 lb. 12 oz. Butter	1 lb. 8 oz. Butter	4 lb. Butter
Shortening	1-1/4 oz. Shortening	5 oz. Shortening			
Egg Yolks		4 oz. Egg Yolks		10 ea. Egg Yolks	
Egg whites	1-1/4 oz. Egg whites				

Roll-in Procedure

Method for laminating fat into dough

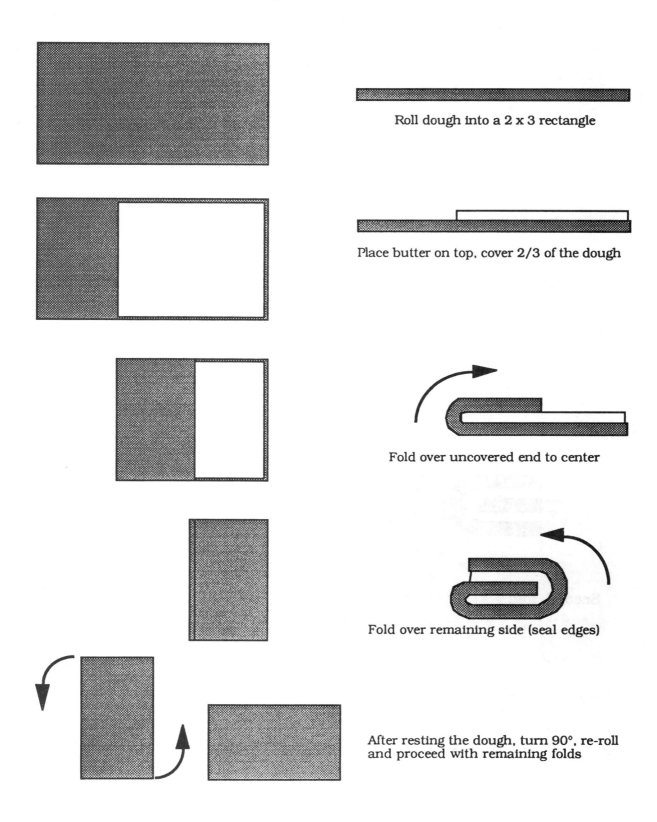

Roll dough into a 2 x 3 rectangle

Place butter on top, cover 2/3 of the dough

Fold over uncovered end to center

Fold over remaining side (seal edges)

After resting the dough, turn 90°, re-roll and proceed with remaining folds

Dough Folding Methods

Three-Fold

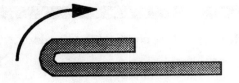

Side view of dough

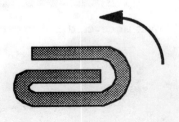

First fold

Second fold

Four-Fold

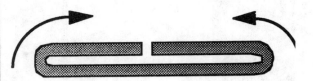

Side view of dough

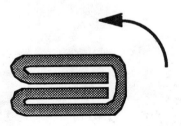

First fold

Second fold